19-36

BLACK HAWK: *an autobiography*

BLACK HAWK

an autobiography

edited by Donald Jackson

University of Illinois Press   *Urbana, 1964*

preface

When this volume is published, the text of the first edition of Black Hawk's autobiography will again be in print after 122 years. It has appeared in several editions since 1833, and one edition, issued in Chicago by the Lakeside Press in 1916, contained some excellent notes and an introduction by Milo Milton Quaife. But much fresh material bearing upon the Black Hawk period has come to light in the thirty-nine years since Quaife's notes were written.

This new edition could not have been prepared without the use of the fine Black Hawk War collection at the Illinois State Historical Library, in Springfield, and without the help of the Library personnel. I am grateful to Harry E. Pratt, state historian, Margaret A. Flint, reference librarian, and Ellen Whitney, who is preparing the Black Hawk War collection for publication and who has been a particularly helpful consultant. The Library will, within the next few years, publish the collection in three volumes; the first volume will contain the muster rolls and payrolls of the Black Hawk War, and the later volumes will consist of documents relating to the campaign.

I wish to thank the staffs of the National Archives; Smithsonian Institution; Chicago Historical Society; Missouri Historical Society; and the State Historical Society of Wisconsin.

The following persons have aided me in various ways: John Francis McDermott, of Washington University, St. Louis; Clyde C. Walton, Jr., of the State University of Iowa; Natalia Belting and Marguerite Pease, of the University of Illinois; John Hauberg, of Rock Island, Illinois; Joe E. Pierce, of Indiana University; Paul Rowe, of Glenwood, Iowa.

January, 1955   *Donald Jackson*

LIST OF SYMBOLS

AGO	Adjutant General's Office.
CHI	Chicago Historical Society. Manuscript and print collections.
ICC	Indian Claims Commission. Sac and Fox Tribes of Oklahoma, *et al.*, v. United States, Docket 83, 1953.
IHI	Illinois State Historical Library. Black Hawk War collection.
MO	Missouri Historical Society.
NA	National Archives.
NA in IHI	National Archives document in Illinois State Historical Library as photostat or microfilm.
OIA	Office of Indian Affairs.
SW	Office of Secretary of War.
WHI	State Historical Society of Wisconsin. Forsyth Papers (Series T) in the Draper collection.

contents

Map of upper Illinois and lower Wisconsin, showing the route of Black Hawk's band during the Black Hawk War. In the shaded area the route was confused and varied, and is not exactly known today.

introduction

Indians were no novelty to Andrew Jackson; he had beaten the Creek braves at Horseshoe Bend and routed the Seminole into Florida country, in those strenuous days before he had turned from soldiering to politics. But since his election to the Presidency it had been necessary for him to deal with Indians in a different way. He was no longer their enemy — he was their Great Father.

As Great Father of all the tribes that had submitted to domination by the government, the President often was required to meet with visiting delegations of chiefs and headmen. Sometimes they came to Washington to discuss land cessions or to sign treaties, and sometimes merely to see for themselves the marvels that civilization had brought to the Eastern shore. Perhaps the little group of men who stood before the President on the morning of April 25, 1833, could not have been called a delegation. They were indeed Indians, transported from St. Louis by steamboat, carriage, and rail. But they were prisoners, not delegates. With rank and prestige gone, they stood before President Jackson representing the defeated band of warriors that had drawn federal troops to the upper Mississippi Valley, in the preceding spring and summer, for the campaign that was called the Black Hawk War.

Their leader was old Black Hawk, known in the language of his people as Makataimeshekiakiak. He was the same age as Jackson (sixty-six by his own tally), a hollow-cheeked, hook-nosed Sauk whose scalp was plucked bald except for a short tuft of hair on top. If he had been wearing his gaudy scalp-lock, the traditional head-dress of animal hair that was designed to stand coarse and plumed upon his head, he would have fulfilled every Easterner's conception of the Savage Redskin.[1] But without it he looked even less warlike than President Jackson, whose gray hair rose erect above his long, stern face and made him seem to be the fiercest man in the room.

Black Hawk was dressed in buckskin and about his shoulders hung a bright blanket. At his side he wore the feathered skin of the sparrow hawk for which he was named, and around the rim of each ear was a row of jingling little baubles. This was the man who, though not a chief, had led a band of horsemen that sent settlers fleeing all along the frontier in Illinois and the territory that is now lower Wisconsin. Though not a chief, he had risen by generalship and fighting zeal to a position of rank among the Sauk. To see that his days of fighting were over was now the purpose of President Jackson and the Department of War.

Standing beside Black Hawk and towering above him was a gloomy associate, a man of ardor and cunning who had given him unfortunate counsel through the years. He was Wabokieshiek or White Cloud (the Indians called him the Prophet), half Winne-bago and half Sauk, who stood more than six feet tall and was inclined, after his winter of confinement, to be rather fat. His face was full and his eyes set deep, and most of the time he frowned. Unlike his companions, he wore his hair long; but what made him even more conspicuous was his black mustache — an adornment that few Indians cared to wear.

He held a pipe that must have been two feet long, decorated with duck feathers, beads, and ribbons. To the officials in the room, and certainly to most of the settlers back in the Mississippi Valley, he was a scoundrel.

---

[1] It was characteristic of the Sauk to pluck or shave their heads except for the tuft to which they fastened the tail of a deer or elk. The headpiece was fastened to their hair by means of thongs and wooden pegs. For good physical descriptions of the Sauk, see Thwaites, 21:122–24, 22:221–24, and Schoolcraft, 215–16.

The third man was Neapope, the Broth, who said very little. Perhaps he knew that he had already said too much in those tense days when he and the Prophet had deceived Black Hawk. Like the Prophet he was a man of fine build, strong and active. The settlers who knew him, and the historians who later were to write of him, were lavish with the adjectives they used; they called him wily, shrewd, bold, talkative, boastful, treacherous, and deceitful. He was a principal Sauk chief, but seemingly content to let Black Hawk do the recruiting and the commanding when a war was in progress. "I and others were principal chiefs, but Black Hawk was the head warrior and older than us and led us," he had said soon after his capture. He had also shown a touch of remorse then, saying, "For myself I have no vices — I do not smoke or drink and I cannot think what could have led me into such bad roads as I have been traveling. . . ." [2] But his total behavior since then had given his captors the impression that he was not completely sorry about his deceit and the agony it had brought to his people.

He had told Black Hawk that the British were going to help the Indians in their campaign to regain their lands. Today it seems highly unlikely that the British would have sent guns, ammunition, and food down from Canada to support Black Hawk's hopeless venture. But Neapope had said they would, so had the Prophet, and Black Hawk had believed it. The Prophet, after all, was a man in contact with the spirit world, and his dreams were not to be ignored.

Three other men completed the group. One was the Prophet's adopted son, of whom history has left us little record. One was Pamaho, or Fast-Swimming Fish, who would not have been brought along had not Wee-sheet, a man of higher rank, been afflicted with "a Pleuristick, or Pulmonary disease" and left behind. And finally there was Nasheaskuk, the Whirling Thunder, eldest son of Black

[2] Testimony of Neapope, Minutes of an Examination of Indian Prisoners, Aug. 20, 1832, NA:AGO in IHI. In referring to Black Hawk, Neapope used the term "head warrior." Black Hawk's status in the tribe is not clearly known. He was not a principal chief, but there are indications that he was a war chief during a part of his lifetime. A principal Sauk chief called him "my head war chief" during a council with British soldiers in the summer of 1815. (Michigan Historical Collections, 16:192–96.)

Hawk. He was destined to become the darling of the Eastern crowds: a big, handsome, story-book Indian, "in nature and figure, a perfect Apollo," according to one delighted journalist.

The Great Father was stern with his children this morning as he told them why they had been brought to Washington. He showed them the clothing they would have to wear instead of their native garments, and then he revealed an unpleasant surprise. He said he was sending them down to Fortress Monroe, at Old Point Comfort, Virginia, to remain until he decided they could go home. In plain words, they were going to spend some more time in jail. They had already whiled away an entire winter in detention at Jefferson Barracks, south of St. Louis. During part of this time they had been in irons. Now they were eager to go free.

It was the frowning Prophet who replied first to the President. He voiced surprise that they were going to be kept away from home still longer. In the first place, they did not feel responsible for starting the war. And, furthermore, their tribes and families back along the Mississippi were now exposed to the ravages of their old enemies, the Sioux and Menominee. To protect and counsel their people, they needed to go home at once.

Black Hawk then expressed his own astonishment at the President's order. He had thought that he had only come to *visit* the Great Father, as Keokuk had once done; and he thought he would be allowed to return as soon as the visit was finished.

The President's answer was summarized in the press the next day:

The president told them, in conclusion, that he was well apprized of the circumstances which led to the disasters alluded to — that it was unnecessary to look back to them — it was his purpose now to secure the observance of peace — to prevent the frontiers from being again stained with the blood of its inhabitants, the peaceful and helpless — that they need feel no uneasiness about their own women and children, they should not suffer from their enemies, the Sioux and Menominees. He meant to compel the red men to be at peace with each other, as well as with their white neighbors — that he had taken measures with this view, and when it was ascertained that they were effectual — when the tribes had learned that the power they attempted to contend with, was equally able and disposed to protect the peaceful and to punish the violence of aggressors — when his information assured him that their people in particular, were convinced of this, and were disposed quietly and in good faith to observe the terms of peace granted to them, then they would be restored to their families. He then gave his hand to the chiefs and dismissed them.[3]

And so the prisoners were taken away to Fortress Monroe. A writer for the *National Intelligencer*, April 30, commented that they had not been aware, until their interview with Jackson, that they were prisoners. They had supposed, he said, that they were simply being brought to hold council with the President. "We hope that it may be deemed compatible with a just and humane policy, to make their duress of short duration."

Because the *Washington Globe* usually was quick to speak up sharply when criticism of Jackson might be implied, it took issue with the *Intelligencer* on this point: "To insinuate that they were deceived and brought here under any false pretence, is utterly untrue. . . . They were in prison, and we believe in irons, held by the consent of their people, and a treaty stipulation. . . . Their consent to come was never asked." [4]

The meeting with the President had been a fortunate one for the Indians. It seems to have drained away the last traces of resentment that Jackson and his aides had felt toward the instigators of the frontier uprising. Obviously these six men, weary of prison life and lonesome for their people, were no longer fit subjects for official vengeance. They were beaten Indians. And before they had reached the gates of Fortress Monroe, the government already had begun the process of sending them home.

Lewis Cass,[5] the Secretary of War, had instructed his Commis-

[3] *Niles' Weekly Register*, 8 (1833) 152.
[4] Issue of May 3, 1833. That the *Globe* consistently supported Jackson in this matter is not surprising; it had been established in 1830 by friends of Jackson and subsidized by an award of public printing. The three men who conducted the paper, Francis P. Blair, Amos Kendall, and John C. Rives, also advised Jackson on political strategy to the extent that they were called his "kitchen cabinet."
[5] Lewis Cass (1782–1866) had been a brigadier general in the War of 1812. He was later governor of the Territory of Michigan, deeply involved with Indian affairs during the eighteen years that he served in that office. As Secretary of War in Jackson's cabinet, 1831–36, he directed the conduct of the campaign against Black Hawk.

sioner of Indian Affairs to send for them in mid-March.[6] Before
the letter could reach the Army people at Jefferson Barracks, Keokuk and other chiefs and braves of the Sauk and Fox tribes had
gone down the river to the Barracks and personally appealed for
the release of all the prisoners who had been taken at the end of
the war.[7] But their appeal, while given strong consideration, was
not sufficient to alter the plans of the War Department; General
Henry Atkinson, in command at Jefferson Barracks, sent off the
six prisoners early in April.[8]

Upon seeing the prisoners and talking with them, Secretary Cass
decided immediately that they ought to be restored to their people.
But apparently he did not wish to take the responsibility alone,
risking an affront to the officials at Jefferson Barracks who were
closer to the situation than he. Perhaps he was keeping in mind
that the governor of Illinois had once recommended that Black
Hawk be held in prison for ten years or longer.[9]

On the day the Indians left Washington for Fortress Monroe,
Commissioner Elbert Herring wrote this letter to General Atkinson:

[6] "The Secretary of War considers it expedient, that Black Hawk, The Prophet,
Napope and We-sheet, together with not exceeding four others, to be selected
by yourself and Genl. Atkinson, and now confined as Hostages at Jefferson Barracks, should be conducted to this place, in the vicinity of which they can be
kept with less danger of escape, and with more comfort to themselves. . . ."
(Herring to Clark, March 16, 1833, NA:OIA.)

[7] In reply, Commissioner Herring sent word to Keokuk through William
Clark: "You will be pleased to inform Keokuk that Black Hawk and his five
associates . . . arrived here in health and are kindly treated — that there is no
intention to injure them, that powerful reasons demand their detention at
present, and at the proper time they will be liberated and returned to their
country." (Herring to Clark, May 4, 1833, NA:OIA.)

[8] Atkinson to Macomb, April 6, 1833, NA:AGO. Henry Atkinson (1782–1842) had
commanded expeditions up the Missouri in 1819 and 1825. Even before the
Black Hawk War he had been no stranger to the Indians of the Mississippi
Valley, having quelled an outbreak among the Winnebago in 1827. The Indians
called him the White Beaver. His debatable generalship in the Black Hawk
campaign is discussed below, on pp. 22–24.

[9] Gen. Winfield Scott concurred in this recommendation. (Scott and Reynolds
to Secretary of War, Sept. 22, 1832, NA:AGO in IHI.) Scott had been the first to
suggest that the hostages be sent to Fortress Monroe, where they would not require a guard. (Scott to Secretary of War, Nov. 19, 1832, NA:SW in IHI.)

I have the honor to inform you that Black Hawk and the other five prisoners arrived here on Monday last April 22 and will this day be conducted
to Fortress Monroe. They appear to be very impatient of restraint, and
are profuse in promises of good conduct in future. I am instructed to
obtain your opinion on the expediency of releasing them, and sending
them to their friends again. Would it or would it not be an advisable
measure, viewing it in its probable consequences, as affecting the interest
and safety of our Citizens, and the feelings and conduct of their own
People? They appear to the Department to be humbled and powerless,
conscious of having done wrong and determined to refrain from hostility
in future; and besides, Keokuck and other Chiefs have pledged their faith
and made themselves responsible for the future good conduct of the
Prisoners.[10]

Both Atkinson and William Clark,[11] the Superintendent of Indian Affairs at St. Louis, replied to Herring's letter. Atkinson
agreed that the prisoners should be brought home, and asked that
they be turned over to Keokuk, "in order that they may be made
to feel a dependence on their Chiefs for their release. . . ."[12]
Clark wrote in a similar vein, saying:

I feel satisfied that all of the least reflection among the Sacs & Foxes, are
fully impressed with the utter folly & hopelessness of contending against
the arms of the UStates, with any combinations Indians are capable of
forming. I therefore think that the Sac prisoners confined at Fortress
Monroe, may be restored to their friends and country without affecting
the interest or safety of our citizens; and their release will not only be
hailed with thankfulness by their own immediate families & friends, but
will also be a gratifying proof to Keokuck and other friendly Chiefs, of
the confidence placed by the Government in their good faith & intentions. . . .[13]

Atkinson and Clark both suggested that the prisoners be brought
back by way of the principal Eastern cities — Baltimore, Philadel-

[10] Herring to Atkinson, April 25, 1833, NA:OIA.
[11] Clark (1770–1838) was territorial governor of Missouri from 1813 to 1820
and superintendent of Indian affairs at St. Louis from 1822 until his death. He
was the younger brother of George Rogers Clark, and in 1803–6 had joined
Meriwether Lewis in the famous expedition from St. Louis to the mouth of the
Columbia River.
[12] Atkinson reminded Herring that he had recommended earlier the release of
all the Indians in custody except Neapope and the Prophet. (Atkinson to Herring, May 20, 1833, NA:OIA.)
[13] Clark to Herring, May 14, 1833, NA:OIA.

phia, and New York — that they might see how futile it was to make war on so powerful a country.

There is nothing to indicate that the Indians were oppressed at Fortress Monroe. The Adjutant General had instructed the commander of the fort that "every proper indulgence be granted the hostages." It was the wish of the President, he said, that they be restricted only to the limits of the garrison, "and that restraints be imposed on them, only so far as may be supposed necessary to guarantee their presence at your Post, until removed by orders from the War Department." [14]

The officers' wives gave them presents, and artists came to paint their portraits.[15] When the time came at last for them to leave, there were expressions of good will on all sides. In thanking Colonel Abraham Eustis, the commander of the fort, Black Hawk said, "We have buried the tomahawk, and the sound of the rifle will hereafter only bring death to the deer and the buffalo. . . . The memory of your friendship will remain till the Great Spirit says it is time for Black Hawk to sing his death-song." [16]

[14] Jones to Eustis, April 25, 1833, NA:AGO.
[15] Sitting for portraits seems to have occupied the prisoners a great deal. Earlier, at Jefferson Barracks, George Catlin had sketched them. Robert M. Sully reportedly spent six weeks at Fortress Monroe, making portraits of Black Hawk, his son, and the Prophet (*Wis. Mag. of Hist.*, 29:289) . Samuel M. Brookes also worked with the prisoners (Hodge, II, 33) , and so did John Wesley Jarvis and Charles Bird King. One King portrait was painted at this time, and a second one was done in 1837 during Black Hawk's second visit to Washington (see Ewers, 470).
Another notable caller at Jefferson Barracks had been Washington Irving, who termed the prisoners "a forlorn crew, emaciated and dejected — the redoubtable chieftain himself, a meagre old man upwards of seventy. He has, however, a fine head, a Roman style of face, and a prepossessing countenance." (Letter of Dec. 18, 1832, quoted in B. Drake, 202.) British traveler Charles Latrobe, who also visited at Jefferson Barracks, said that Black Hawk "drooped like the bird whose name he bore, when caged and imprisoned." And Latrobe little thought that six months later he would see the old Indian "alive and in freedom, on his 'progress' through the Atlantic cities . . . wondering at all, and wondered at by all." Latrobe, I, 116). Maximilian, Prince of Wied-Neuwied, stopped by on his journey to the Indian tribes of the West.
[16] B. Drake, 204. Black Hawk's quoted utterances during the tour are sometimes flowery and sometimes straightforward and simple. This is probably a result of uneven reporting rather than uneven interpreting. Black Hawk himself was unhappy with the interpreter, Charles St. Vrain, who had accompanied

The party left Fortress Monroe on the evening of June 4, escorted by Brevet Major John Garland, and from the moment they passed the gates they were celebrities and tourists — though still officially prisoners. First they visited Norfolk and the Navy yard at Gosport. They inspected the *Delaware*, a 74-gun ship of the line, and signed in at a Norfolk hotel. On the balcony of this hotel the Prophet was inspired to make the first of several public addresses he was to deliver on the tour. To the crowd outside his hotel, he is quoted as saying: "We will go home with peaceable dispositions towards our white brethren, and make our conduct hereafter, more satisfactory to them." [17]

Leaving the Chesapeake Bay area June 5 aboard the steamer *Columbus*, the party arrived late the next morning at Baltimore. They had planned to go directly to Philadelphia, but the press reported that Black Hawk, feeling his years and the strain of recent days, was not quite well. So they all checked in at the Fountain Inn on Light Street.[18]

The unexpected stay at Baltimore brought Black Hawk once more into the presence of President Jackson. The President was beginning his own tour of the seaboard cities, and on June 6 he left Washington for Baltimore. He had more than Indians on his mind that day; he wrote a letter to Vice-President Van Buren, saying, "My own health is not good, I want relaxation from business and rest, but where can I get rest. I fear not on this earth." [19] It was hardly the mood in which to begin a demanding series of public appearances.

On the night of June 6 the President and Black Hawk were present in the same theater, and on the following day they exchanged greetings. "You will see," said the President, "that our young men are as numerous as the leaves in the woods. What can you do against us? You may kill a few women and children, but such a

him from Jefferson Barracks. He criticizes St. Vrain's skill twice in the autobiography.

[17] B. Drake, 206.

[18] Samuel G. Drake (p. 663) says that the warm weather and the crowds about the hotel caused the party to retire to Fort McHenry, about three miles below Baltimore.

[19] Barrett, V, 106.

force would be soon sent against you, as would destroy your whole tribe. . . . We desire your prosperity and improvement. . . . and I pray the Great Spirit to give you a smooth path and fair sky to return." [20]

The omnipresence of the Great Father must have given the Indian tourists reason to wonder. For when they reached Philadelphia three days later, Jackson had been parading through the streets on horseback. And when they arrived at New York, he was there. He did not see them after the Baltimore meeting, but he probably reflected now and then upon the poor planning that had resulted in parallel routes. The crowd that gathered to see him in Philadelphia was nearly matched by the turnout for the Indians.

With two celebrities as different as Jackson and Black Hawk in the area, comparisons were inevitable. One commentary in the press ran this way:

The tall, thin figure, the white locks and the white horse of the one were considered as nearly equalled in interest by the red face, the blanket and the beads, and the immovable countenance of the other; and a large portion of the American people had, at the same instant, the pleasure of beholding him, beneath whose arms so many of the sons of the forest had fallen, and whose laurels had been bathed in so much Cherokee, Chickasaw and Seminole blood; and him, also, who had upheld to the utmost of his power, the falling fortunes of his tribe.[21]

In Philadelphia Major Garland headquartered his wards at the Congress Hall Hotel. He took them to the mint, the waterworks, and the theaters. "The whole of the deputation . . . were taken to the Cherry Hill prison, and shown the manner in which white men punish," said the *United States Gazette*, June 29. To six Indians who had just spent a winter imprisoned at Jefferson Barracks, this must have been the least informative aspect of their tour.

Black Hawk probably had one or more meetings with Colonel

[20] *Niles' Weekly Register*, 8 (1833) 256. Jackson's avowed policy was always to tell an Indian a straight story. He once wrote to Col. John D. Terrill, who had been made special agent to prepare the Chickasaw for a cession of lands: "With these hints I shall only add that you should be careful to promise nothing to them, but what you will religiously perform, or they will say to you, you lye too much. Nothing will defeat a negotiation with the Indians so soon as the discovery of an attempt to deceive them." (Barrett, III, 309.)
[21] *American Quarterly Review*, 35 (1834) 426.

Thomas S. McKenney in Philadelphia. The former Commissioner
of Indian Affairs had been granted permission to conduct some
interviews in connection with a book he was later to publish with
Judge James Hall, *History of the Indian Tribes of North America*.[22]

The Indians were dumfounded everywhere by what they saw.
Major Garland reported, "It was with difficulty they could believe
their own senses, when these populous cities and the immense
crowds of people, assembled in them to pay their respects to the
chief Magistrate of the Nation, were placed before their view; they
had not formed even a distant conception of the extent and population of the United States; their information on this subject did
not extend beyond Buffalo on the Lakes and St. Louis on the
Mississippi." [23]

Black Hawk is said to have expressed surprise "at seeing the
white people of Philadelphia at the Theatre call for 'Jim Crow' the
fourth time!" [24] But he could not have felt much surprise, by this
time, at the remorseful oratory of the Prophet, who rose to tell a
theater audience, "I would cheerfully take you all by the hand,
but you are too numerous. . . . We pledge ourselves, as representatives of our nation, never again to wage war with the white men
of America, and do sincerely hope you will keep back the rifle on
your part, while on ours, we will bury the tomahawk in the
earth." [25]

The newspapers grew accustomed to the Indians. Soon the emphasis in news stories was less upon the serious aspects of the tour
and more upon bits of gossip about what the men said and did.
Some of the papers began to run such matter under the heading,
Blackhawkiana. They referred to Black Hawk's son as Tommy
Hawk, and quoted expressions in broken English that he and the
others were said to have used. "I lazee," for example, and "pretty
squaws." One news story described Pamaho as "a good-natured old

[22] Sargent to Secretary of War, May 31, 1833, and Herring to Garland, June 3,
1833, NA:OIA.
[23] Garland to Secretary of War, Oct. 5, 1833, NA:OIA.
[24] *National Intelligencer*, June 20, 1833.
[25] Ibid., June 15, 1833.

brave, who bears his misfortunes with a philosophy worthy of the ancients." And of Black Hawk, another said, "His eye is small, black, and as piercing as that of the Missouri hawk from which he derives his name."

The *National Intelligencer* reprinted on June 29 a waggish item which it said had appeared in the *Courier and Enquirer*, of New York, purporting to be a letter that Black Hawk had sent "to his illustrious squaw, *Debikit Ikibis*, or Star of Night." In it, Black Hawk expressed the belief that "all this admiration is owing to my having killed a few Long Knives, and burnt up some of the women and children in their wigwams. . . ."

A pamphleteer, anxious to be dramatic even if not accurate, printed the following account of Black Hawk's behavior at a social function:

Being invited to a ball at Philadelphia, he was pressed to join in the dance, whereupon he sent for his dancing dress, consisting of a Buffaloes hide with the horns and tail on.

In this costume he commenced such an outrageous system of capering accompanied with such hideous yells as he uses in his own native forests, that the admirers of nature and simplicity became greatly alarmed. The fidlers got out of tune, the ladies screamed, and a celebrated dandy burst his boiler, that is to say his corsets, which was a source of great merriment to the party, and more particularly to the red skin warrior. . . .

Among the admiring women was one who presented him with a toma-hawk. Black Hawk patted her on the head and observed to his son, "what a beautiful head for scalping." How must the female bosom shudder at such an expression from him (though at the time a prisoner) who have scalped of the most promising youths, among whom where [*sic*] not only many interesting young ladies, but even the lovely infant upon its mothers breast has shared the same merciless fate.[26]

For New Yorkers, June 14 was not only the day that President Jackson and Black Hawk both were in town; it was also the day the balloon went up. At 5 o'clock in the afternoon, just as the steamer carrying the Indians was approaching the dock, occurred "the ascent of Mr. Durant (in a balloon)." Always looking for a line or two to print under *Blackhawkiana*, newspapermen questioned the Indians about their reactions. The *Boston Evening Transcript*,

[26] *An Account of the Indian Chief Black Hawk* . . . (Philadephia, 1833).

June 17, printed these quotes: from Black Hawk, "That man is brave — don't think he will ever get back"; and from his son, "I think he can see the English country." Black Hawk's son was popular with the women of New York. An earlier observer had once said of him, "Had his countenance not been wanting in that peculiar expression which emanates from a cultivated intellect and which education alone can give, we could have looked upon him as the living personification of our *beau ideal* of manly beauty." [27] The absence of cultivated intellect did not deter several women, who, "admiring the noble form and handsome face of young Black Hawk, warmly kissed him!" [28]

The visit to New York was a repetition of the Philadelphia experience; there was a round of sightseeing which included the theaters, public gardens, and the arsenal (to show once more the armed strength of the palefaces). The group had been taken to the Exchange Hotel on Broad Street after crowds prevented their stopping at Holt's, and the newspapers reported highlights of their week's schedule as follows: Saturday, Bowery Theater; Monday, Castle Garden; Tuesday, Park Theater; Wednesday, Niblo's Theater; Thursday, Richmond Hill Theater; Friday, Vauxhall Garden.

In their hotel suite the Indians were visited by prominent New York citizens. As he accepted a pair of topaz earrings for his wife, presented by John A. Graham, Black Hawk said, "Brother, we like your talk. We will be friends. We like the white people. They are very kind to us. We shall not forget it. Your counsel is good. We shall attend to it. Your valuable present shall go to my squaw. We shall always be friends." [29]

Major Garland had planned to take the group to Boston; but by this time Black Hawk was tired of city life and the continual round of speeches and official visits. The Major was probably not anxious to exhibit his troupe again in competition with President Jackson, who was working his way toward Boston. The Boston visit was canceled and on June 22 the Indians left New York aboard a steamer bound for Albany.

[27] *Niles' Weekly Register*, 8 (1833) 182.
[28] Ibid., 282.
[29] B. Drake, 212.

They had not escaped from gaping crowds. When the boat arrived at Albany, thousands of citizens were lining the shore. Newspaper accounts gave the impression that these people were merely
curious onlookers, straining to see a celebrity. But Major Garland,
in a letter to the Secretary of War, revealed a different impression.
When he had moved on to Buffalo, he wrote:

Since I took charge of the Indian prisoners at Fort Monroe, I met with
kind and hospitable people, until my arrival at Albany, where, for the
first time, the party were unduly assailed, by a mob assembled to witness
the landing of Black Hawk. The sight was really appalling both from the
number of the mob and its ruffian like appearance. I fortunately met with
some few gentlemen with whose assistance the party reached a carriage
in safety, the driver, however, was pelted with brick bats in trying to force
his way through the crowd. I determined under all the circumstances of
the case to make a speedy retreat and accordingly drove, under cover of
the dark, to Schenecktady, where we arrived with whole bones and empty
pockets for in passing through the crowd of Albany ruffians, my wallet
containing $100 was extracted from its hiding place by some dexterous
cut purse. This unpleasant affair caused me to move more rapidly through
the country than I had intended to do. The people of the towns and villages do not appear satisfied with the rapidity of my movement. The fact
is, both the Indians and myself are heartily tired of crowds. . . .[30]

When the party boarded a steamer at Buffalo on June 30 for the
trip through the Lakes, one of the passengers was William Armiger
Scripps, of London, a publisher traveling west to visit relatives. In
his diary he described Black Hawk as "dressed in a short blue
frock coat, white hat and red leggins tied around below the knee
with garters. . . . His shirt not very clean. . . . His nose perfo-
rated very wide between the nostrils, so as to give it the appearance
of the upper and under mandibles of a hawk. He wears light col-
ored leather gloves, and a walking stick with a tassel." Scripps reported that Nasheaskuk, the son, "makes great use of a silver
toothpick," and that he "has many ornaments about him and little
bells that jingle as he walks."

Fretful old Black Hawk apparently did not enjoy this leg of the
journey very much. Scripps said he worried lest his hat should blow

[30] Garland to Secretary of War, June 30, 1833, NA:OIA. A month of travel still
remained.

off, got out of bed two or three times during the night, complained of the heat, and "was half inclined to dispense with his mattress." [31]

The Indians visited Detroit (where they were allegedly burned in effigy) [32] and then journeyed via Lake Huron to Mackinac and down to Green Bay. At Green Bay they embarked in an open boat and went up the Fox River and down the Wisconsin River to its junction with the Mississippi. They stopped at Prairie du Chien, and since the family of the Prophet and his adopted son were above that place, the two were released. The rest of the prisoners were taken down the Mississippi to Fort Armstrong, at Rock Island, where they were freed after a council which Major Garland held with the chiefs and headmen of the Sauk and Fox tribes. [33]

Black Hawk's own version of the Eastern tour is given near the end of his autobiography, pp. 143–50.

Summary of the War

To understand why the American government had put these men in prison and in irons, we must review the events that began to occur in the preceding spring.

The Black Hawk War of 1832 was barely a war. It lasted just fifteen weeks. It cost the lives of but seventy settlers and soldiers. [34] And the invading force was not a band of marauding redskins on the warpath, but a migration which included Indian women and children. They were surly migrators, it is true, and they were ready for trouble. The warriors were armed and determined. Black Hawk, deceived by chiefs and medicine men, thought he was leading his people to an alliance with the Winnebago, the Potawatomi, and even the British in Canada — an alliance that would help him rescue from the white settlers the site of his ancestral village and the cornfields that surrounded it. But he did not expect to fight

[31] From handwritten excerpts in the Illinois Historical Survey, Urbana, transcribed from James E. Scripps, *Memorials of the Scripps Family* (Detroit, 1891), a privately printed book issued in 100 copies.
[32] B. Drake, 213–14.
[33] Garland to Secretary of War, Oct. 5, 1833, NA:OIA.
[34] Not all of these deaths can be attributed to Black Hawk's people. Some of the killings occurred many miles from the war area.

unless attacked. He could not know that he was leading his people to starvation and slaughter.

A notable aspect of the Black Hawk War is the number of public figures and future public figures that were assembled for a time in the Rock River country of the Mississippi Valley. There were future presidents and statesmen, future generals, soldiering beside national heroes who had survived the War of 1812. Among the names on the muster rolls:

Abraham Lincoln, a captain of Illinois Mounted Volunteers in the first army of citizens, and a private in two later companies.

Colonel Zachary Taylor, leading troops in the field and later commanding the Fort Crawford garrison at Prairie du Chien.

Jefferson Davis, a lieutenant selected to escort the captured Black Hawk down the river to prison.

Major General Winfield Scott, hampered by cholera, who would later become General in Chief of the United States Army.

Colonel David Twiggs, who lost most of his command from cholera, and who would defect to the South in the Civil War — taking with him his troops and valuable supplies.

Lieutenant Robert Anderson, the Assistant Inspector General of troops in the field, who would distinguish himself at the defense of Fort Sumter.

Lieutenant Albert Sidney Johnston, aide-de-camp to the commanding general, who would command the Confederate forces at the Battle of Shiloh.

Political figures, present and future, were everywhere. In addition to Governor John Reynolds, commanding the militia, the volunteer horsemen included such future Illinois governors as Thomas Ford, Joseph Duncan, and Thomas Carlin. Colonel Henry Dodge would one day become governor of Wisconsin. Orville H. Browning, a private in Whiteside's Brigade, would become a United States senator and Secretary of the Interior.

An official account of the Black Hawk War appears in a report from the Commanding General of the Army to the Secretary of War, submitted in November, 1832. It is a report that history has amended in some respects, but it is concise, predominantly accurate, and is presented here as a useful outline of the campaign.

In the month of March last, intelligence was received that the Menomonees, exasperated by a wanton and unprovoked attack and murder committed by the Sacs and Foxes on an unarmed party of their tribe, near the Prairie du Chien, in the month of August previous, meditated a descent on those tribes, with the intention of taking revenge for that outrage. Apprehending that this movement would lead to a general war among the Indians on the northwestern frontiers, General Atkinson was directed to proceed to Rock Island with the effectual force at Jefferson barracks, and demand of the Sacs and Foxes the surrender of the persons concerned in the murder of the Menomonees; at the same time to station troops, to be drawn from the posts on the Upper Mississippi and from Fort Winnebago, at points on the Mississippi, from which they might intercept the Menomonees in their contemplated descent, turn them back, and inform them that the government had determined to see that justice should be done. While these measures were in progress a large party of Sacs and Foxes under Black Hawk, among whom were those concerned in the attack and murder of the Menomonees, crossed the Mississippi at the Yellow Banks, and, uniting with the Prophet's band of Winnebagoes, in all about 800 or 1,000 strong,[35] took a position on Rock river, and assumed an attitude of defiance. Under these circumstances it was not in the power of the friendly Sac and Fox Indians to surrender the murderers as demanded, although they had expressed a willingness so to do. Thus situated, General Atkinson did not conceive that the force under his command was sufficient to justify him in attacking the hostile party, lest an unsuccessful attempt should add to their numbers the wavering and disaffected, and especially as they had not as yet committed any act of hostility, although they evinced a desire to make war upon the whites.

The people settled on the frontiers of Illinois, alarmed at the appearance of so large a band of Indians in their immediate vicinity, with indications of no friendly feelings, fled from their farms into the interior of the State. The governor of the State ordered out in haste, and for no definite period, a brigade of militia, to assemble on Rock river. These troops, after a march across the country to Ottawa in quest of the Indians, became anxious for their discharge, which the governor granted, retain-

[35] In his journal, April 10, 1832 (in IHI), Lt. Albert S. Johnston reported that "this band consisted of 4 or 500 well appointed horsemen besides men and boys employed in transporting the canoes, capable of bearing arms, making an active & efficient force of between 5 & 600 the whole, men, women & children amounting to above two thousand souls." General Atkinson, borrowing Johnston's phrasing but boosting his figures, described the band as "amounting to 500 well appointed horsemen besides men and boys employed in navigating their canoes, capable of bearing arms forming an efficient body of between six and seven hundred men." (Report to the Adjutant General, Nov. 19, 1832, in IHI.) Even with the Winnebago who joined Black Hawk after he had crossed the river, the total of fighting men probably was not much more than 600.

ing of those who were discharged, and volunteered for a further term
of twenty days, enough to form six companies. In the meantime, however, instructions were sent to General Atkinson, authorizing him to call
on the governor of Illinois for such a militia force as would, with the
regular troops under his command, enable him to act efficiently. Accordingly, three thousand mounted volunteers were ordered into the field by
the governor, on the requisition of General Atkinson, and assembled at
Fort Deposit, near Ottawa, about the 18th of June, where they were organized. Towards the latter part of that month the campaign was opened
with these troops and about four hundred regulars, then at Dixon's Ferry,
on the Rock river. Black Hawk, finding himself unable to cope with so
large a force, retired into the swamps and fastnesses, sending out at the
same time parties of active warriors to pick up stragglers, and to attack
defenceless settlements. In this manner he annoyed the people residing
in that part of Michigan [36] called the Mining District, and murdered a
number of our citizens, men, women, and children. The people, in different directions of the exposed country, fortified themselves, and by occa-
sional sallies inflicted punishment on these ruthless savages. With a view
to cover the exposed settlements in the countries of Jo Daviess, in Illinois,
and Iowa, in Michigan, and to intercept the Indians, should they attempt
to cross in that direction, General Atkinson detached one brigade into
that country; and, with the remaining force under his command, consisting of four hundred and fifty regulars and about two thousand mounted
volunteers, moved in the direction of the Four Lakes in pursuit of the
main body of the Indians, which was then understood to be encamped
in a strong position in the swamps, about ten miles above Lake Goosh-
we-hawn [Koshkonong]. General Atkinson halted his army on White
Water creek for the purpose of ascertaining the exact position of the
Indians. After being frustrated in his attempts to discover them, he was
obliged to disperse his mounted volunteers on account of the low state
of the supplies intended for their subsistence. One portion, under General Henry, was sent to Hamilton's, a distance of forty-five miles; and
another, under General Dodge, to Fort Winnebago, a distance of thirty-
five miles — two points where provisions were expected to be in deposit.
Having received the supply of provisions, Generals Henry and Dodge returned to the swamp, on the west side of Rock river, with a view of obtaining some information concerning the enemy. At the same time
General Atkinson, with the regular troops, and General Alexander's
brigade of mounted volunteers, moved up on the east side of the swamp
with the same intention. Black Hawk, finding himself likely to be pressed

[36] In the present state of Wisconsin, which was then a part of the Michigan Territory. A Wisconsin Territory was organized in 1836, and Wisconsin became a
state in 1848.

on all sides, and being no longer able to supply himself with the means of subsistence, broke up his camp and marched towards the Mississippi. The volunteers under Generals Dodge and Henry, discovering the enemy's trail, pursued it, and came up with him on the 21st of July, on the left bank of the Wisconsin, about twenty miles below Fort Winnebago, where an engagement ensued, which lasted until 7 o'clock in the afternoon, during which the Indians found means to convey across the Wisconsin their non-combatants and baggage. The volunteers having marched forty miles on the day of the action, exposed to the rain for more than six hours, and their arms being wet and out of order, were not in a condition to continue the pursuit that night. The next morning they found that the Indians had crossed the river in bark canoes, which they had on the emergency of the occasion prepared. The loss on the part of the volunteers was one killed and seven wounded; that of the Indians, it was found afterwards, amounted to sixty-eight killed, together with a large number wounded.

The moment General Atkinson was informed that the volunteers were on the trail of the enemy he marched in pursuit, and arrived at the Blue Mounds, near the Wisconsin, where he was joined on the evening of the 23d of July by the volunteers under Generals Dodge and Henry, who had retired to that place for a supply of provisions. The army being refreshed and provisioned, a select body, consisting of four hundred regulars under Colonel Taylor, of the first regiment of infantry, and detachments of Generals Henry, Dodge, Posey, and Alexander's mounted volunteers, amounting in all to thirteen hundred men, crossed the Wisconsin on the 27th and 28th of July under General Atkinson, took up the trail of the enemy, and pursued it by forced marches through a broken and difficult country until the morning of the 2d of August, when they came up with the main body on the left bank of the Mississippi, opposite the mouth of the Iowa, which they attacked, defeated, and dispersed, with a loss on the part of the Indians of upwards of one hundred and fifty men killed. Many were slain in attempting to cross the river; others escaped in that direction; while the remainder, among whom was Black Hawk, fled into the interior of the Winnebago country. Our loss in this engagement was comparatively small, being only five regulars killed and four wounded; of the volunteers, two officers and thirteen privates wounded.

On information being received by General Atkinson that the Indians had quitted the swamps in the neighborhood of the Four Lakes and marched towards the Mississippi, he despatched instructions to the commanding officer of Prairie du Chien to take measures to intercept them, should they attempt to descend the Wisconsin or cross the Mississippi. In consequence of these instructions a guard and an armed flat were stationed on the Wisconsin about twenty-five miles from its junction with the Mississippi; by which means a number of those who escaped from the engagement on the Wisconsin were killed or captured. A steamboat in the employ of the quartermaster's department, armed with a field piece, and manned with about twenty men, was despatched up the Mississippi to watch the motions of the Indians, and on the 1st of August discovered a large body of them on the left bank making preparations to cross the river. The Indians at first attempted to deceive our party by declaring themselves to be Winnebagoes, and displaying white flags, at the same time inviting them to land. But the officer in command being aware of their intentions fired upon them, and killed twenty-five of their number. The fire was smartly returned by the Indians, but without effect. This circumstance fortunately checked the Indians in their attempt to cross the river, and led to the action of the 2d of August.

The enemy being thus cut up and dispersed, General Atkinson conceived it unnecessary to pursue him further. He, therefore, fell down with his force to Prairie du Chien; from which place were despatched, on both sides of the Mississippi, parties of friendly Indians to follow the fugitives and bring them in; and it is believed that not an individual composing the band of Black Hawk has escaped being either killed or captured.

From the information which had been received at the seat of Government of the state of things on frontier, and with the desire of putting a speedy termination to the war, without calling for any additional militia force, orders were given on the 16th of June for all the force that could be spared from the seaboard, the lakes, and the Lower Mississippi, to repair at once to the scene of action, and Major General Scott was directed to assume the general conduct of the war. Under this order, nine companies of artillery, equipped as infantry, drawn from Forts Monroe and McHenry, and from the harbor of New York, with a detachment of two hundred and eight recruits from the last-mentioned place, and nine companies of infantry from the posts on the lakes, amounting in all to upwards of one thousand men, took up their march for Chicago, near the head of Lake Michigan, the point of rendezvous. Besides this force, two companies of infantry from Baton Rouge, Louisiana, proceeded, by the way of the Mississippi, to the headquarters of General Atkinson.

From the promptness with which this movement was begun, and the rapidity with which it was conducted, reasonable hopes were entertained that the campaign would be of but short duration, and the hostile Indians completely subdued. Unfortunately, however, the cholera was just at this time making its way into the United States from Canada, and infected our troops while on board the steamboats in their passage up the lakes; and such was the rapidity with which this disease spread among them, that in a few days the whole of the force sent by the lakes was rendered incapable of taking the field. Some were landed at Fort Gratiot, others were stopped at Detroit, while the principal part reached Chicago in a most deplorable condition. Of the six companies of artillery which left Fort Monroe, five companies arrived at Chicago, a distance of eighteen hundred miles, in the short space of eighteen days — a rapidity which is believed to be unprecedented in military movements. The loss by cholera in that detachment alone was equal to one out of every three men. General Scott reached Chicago with the first detachment on the 10th of July, where he learned that General Atkinson, with his army, was at Lake Goosh-we-hawn, about eighty miles distant. Here the general found himself in a most perplexing predicament; only a part of his troops had arrived, and they dreadfully afflicted with the cholera. The remainder, which he daily expected, without knowing the cause of their delay, did not appear. He made General Atkinson acquainted with his arrival and orders, but dared not approach him with troops infected with a disorder that might, by being communicated to the army in the field, render the force of General Atkinson, like his own, unfit to prosecute the war, and thereby defeat the very object for the accomplishment of which he had come. Under this painful anxiety, General Scott directed General Atkinson to continue his operations without reference to him, professing, at the same time, the greatest confidence in his ability to bring the war to a successful issue, if the means at his disposal would enable him to do so. General Scott, however, after waiting a reasonable time, and not finding it possible to bring his troops into the field, left Colonel Eustis in command of them, with orders to march in the direction of the enemy as soon as it would be prudent to move, and proceeded himself to join General Atkinson. At Galena he received intelligence of the decisive action of the 2d of August. He thence proceeded to Prairie du Chien, and having made all the necessary arrangements for bringing the Indians who had commenced the war within his power, he retired to Rock Island to enter into negotiations with those of the Sac and Fox Indians, who took no part in the war, and the other tribes interested in the settlement of a peace. The troops under Colonel Eustis, in the meantime, marched across the country to Rock river, and were useful in making the necessary arrangements to give effect to the meeting of the Indians. Impressed with the folly of opposing the government, and convinced of the impropriety of the conduct of those who were the aggressors, the several tribes yielded to an accommodation, at once beneficial to themselves, and satisfactory, it is to be hoped, to the United States. Black Hawk and a number of chiefs are held as hostages under the treaty; the rest of the prisoners were returned to their respective tribes.

The war being concluded, the volunteers were discharged, and the several detachments of regular troops were ordered to their respective quarters, except two companies of the 4th regiment of artillery, which remain to garrison Fort Gratiot, on Lake Huron.[37]

Nothing in the report shows the impatience with which the War Department viewed General Atkinson's activities in the slow-moving campaign. When the delays and indecision had stretched the pursuit of the Indians to eight weeks, the Acting Secretary of War sent a withering criticism to the General: "I am directed by the President to say, that he views with utter astonishment, and deep regret, this state of things . . . the President had a right to anticipate promptness and decision of action, and the capture, or death of Black Hawk, the principal agent in the work of death and desolation. Some one is to blame in this matter, but upon whom it is to fall, is at present unknown to the Department." [38]

This state of affairs led the government to send Major General Winfield Scott (1786–1866) into the field. He had distinguished himself in the War of 1812, rising from the rank of lieutenant colonel to that of brevet major general after his successes at Chippewa and Lundy's Lane. His greatest repute was still to come, in the Mexican War, where his reputation for boldness in battle was to be reaffirmed. He was also to serve for twenty years, after 1841, as supreme commander of the Army.

But because of the cholera outbreak, Scott could do little against Black Hawk. Atkinson was always in direct charge of the troops, and Washington officials continued to fret about his inadequacy. General Macomb wrote to the President, July 24, that Atkinson's latest report was "by no means satisfactory." He said that Atkinson seemed to despair of bringing the Indians to action. "I have caused copies of the dispatches . . . to be made out," Macomb wrote, "in order that you may more clearly see the details which I think cannot be satisfactory to you, especially the implied willingness of

[37] *American State Papers*, Ind. Affairs, I, 29–31. Portions of the report at the beginning and end, not pertaining to the campaign, are omitted. The report was signed by the Commanding General of the Army, Maj. Gen. Alexander Macomb (1782–1841). He had become Adjutant General in 1812, then had commanded troops during the War of 1812. In 1828 he became senior major general and the Commanding General of the Army, a position he was to hold until his death in 1841.
[38] Robb to Atkinson, June 12, 1832, in IHI. The letter was approved by the President.

General Atkinson to await the arrival of General Scott instead of pursuing the Indians and obliging them to try the fate of war." [39]

Atkinson's conduct of the war finally won Scott's approval. A few days after the Bad Axe encounter, Scott wrote to the Secretary of War that "The persevering ardor both of the general & the troops under unusual difficulties & privations, richly merited the success which has been won." [40] But some of General Atkinson's other associates were less willing to forget what they considered his past blunders and those of his superiors. During the winter Zachary Taylor wrote a long commentary on the war to Quartermaster General Thomas Sidney Jesup, in which he said:

In relation to the indian War, I was under the impression untill the receipt of your letter, that it might be attributed to Genl. Atkinson's not having the necessity [*sic*] authority vested in him, of making such dispositions with the troops under his comd. as might be necessary for the safety of the frontier entrusted to his protection, without special orders from the Genl. in chief of the Army; For it must not only have been known to Genl. A. but to the Comdg. Genl. at Washington, for several months previous to Black Hawk & his band crossing to the east side of the Mississippi that thos Indians were in a high state of excitement, & I again repeat had the garrison of Fort Armstrong been re-enforced as could, & ought to have been, with three or four companies from Jefferson Barracks the moment the Mississippi was clear of ice (which was the last of March) there would have been no indian War, & consequently the reputation of the nation would have been saved — There has been an error some where, but how or by whom it has been committed it is not for me to say, & my only wish now is, that we may profit by past blunders —

Taylor then criticized Atkinson's generalship in two specific instances:

I thought at the time I joined the Genl. & still am of the opinion he ought not to have permitted the indians to have ascended rock River, with their fleet of canoes, with their women, children, & baggage of various kinds, including (by report) large quantities of corn, & dried meat, without making the attempt to stop them. . . . Besides that disgraceful affair of Stillmans [see pp. 122–27] ought not to have occured, the Genl. ought to have prevented it, for I am decidedly of opinion that, that attack made on the indians, brought on the war, for there is but little doubt in

[39] Macomb to Jackson, July 24, 1832, typed copy in CHI.
[40] Aug. 10, 1832, NA:SW in IHI.

my mind had the regular troops overtaken them, at any rate in conjunction with the Militia then in the field, before any blood had been shed, they would have been removed back to the West side of the Mississippi, without there being a gun fired. . . .[41]

General Atkinson was painfully conscious of such criticism when he submitted a long report to the Adjutant General a few weeks after the war. He said he understood "that an impression existed or perhaps exists at this time, at Washington that I had it in my power last spring to have prevented Black Hawk from crossing the Mississippi. . . ." He pointed out that Black Hawk had crossed the river more than 300 miles above him, and that he "had it not in my power by previous advices, or by the then existing state of things, to prevent his crossing, or to arrest his march."

The General complained about Major Stillman's "precipitate movement" and about the dispersal of the first army of volunteers before any important fighting had been done, and he concluded, "If it should be thought I called for too large a militia force, I must remark, that I was then under the impression, which has been fully confirmed by subsequent events, that nothing but a show of a heavy body of troops in the heart of the country occupied by the enemy, would prevent his being joined by a large number of Winnebagoes and Pottowatimies, swelling his number to some 1800 or 2000, and probably more." [42]

Is the Autobiography a Hoax?

Since the first appearance of the autobiography in 1833, its accuracy, authenticity, and style have been both praised and damned. The fault that critics find with it is usually expressed in one or more of these comments: Black Hawk didn't dictate it; the facts are

[41] Taylor to Jesup, Dec. 4, 1832, quoted in Holman, 305–15. Taylor had been none too happy with the performance of the Illinois volunteers, either. He had written to Atkinson, during the war, "The more I see of the militia the less confidence I have in their effecting any thing of importance. . . ." (June 2, 1832, IHI.) Zachary Taylor (1784–1850) had served in the War of 1812 as a captain and major. Later, as a major general in the Mexican War, he was to lead his outnumbered troops victoriously against Santa Anna at Buena Vista. He died in 1849, a year after his inauguration as the twelfth president of the United States. His daughter, Sara Knox Taylor, married young Jefferson Davis in 1835.
[42] Atkinson to Jones, Nov. 19, 1832, in IHI.

garbled; no Indian would talk that way; no Indian would ever think of dictating his life story; LeClaire, the interpreter, was an unreliable halfbreed.

The conflicting judgments can be shown best by quotation. The *North American Review*, January, 1835, ran a review of the book which contained this passage on pp. 69–70:

It is almost the only one we have ever read, in which we feel perfect confidence, that the author sincerely believes that every thing he has set down is the truth, the whole truth, and nothing but the truth. That it is the *bona fide* work of Black Hawk, we have the respectable testimony of Antoine Le Clair, the government interpreter for the Sacs and Foxes, and what (as we have not the honor of being acquainted with that gentleman,) we deem more conclusive, the intrinsic evidence of the work itself. We will venture to affirm, and (having long dwelt among the aborigines, we conceive ourself entitled to do so,) that no one but a Sac Indian could have written or dictated such a composition. No white man, however great his ability may be, could have executed a work so thoroughly and truly Indian. Many of the facts therein contained are, moreover, known to us to be true, and of many others we have the testimony of the oral tradition of the country. We think, therefore, we may say that the authenticity of the work is unquestionable. . . . The only drawback upon our credence is the intermixture of courtly phrases, and the figures of speech, which our novelists are so fond of putting into the mouths of Indians. These are, doubtless, to be attributed to the bad taste of Black Hawk's amanuensis.

A contrary opinion appeared in 1854 when ex-Governor Thomas Ford published his *History of Illinois*. In a note on p. 110, referring to the autobiography, he said:

This work has misled many. Black Hawk knew but little, if anything, about it. In point of fact, it was got up from the statements of Mr. Antoine Le Clere and Col. Davenport, and was written by a printer, and was never intended for anything but a catch-penny publication. Mr. Le Clere was a half-breed Indian interpreter. . . .

More recent critics have included the government attorneys participating in hearings before the Indian Claims Commission in Washington, August, 1953. They argued that the Sauk and Fox, seeking payment for lands taken from them in 1804, were basing some of their testimony upon statements in the Black Hawk autobiography — a book which history had already discredited.[43]

[43] Mimeographed testimony, Sac and Fox Indian Tribes of Oklahoma vs. U. S.,

Skepticism such as this is understandable when one considers
the complicated way in which the book was created. According to
its proprietors it was dictated by Black Hawk, translated into English by the interpreter, and put into manuscript form by its editor.
The difficulties of thus getting the revelations of an Indian into
print, with faithfulness to fact and style, are apparent.

Antoine LeClaire said that Black Hawk approached him in
August, 1833, with the desire to tell his life story. It is quite likely
that he was given the idea while touring in the East. If Black Hawk
were to make such a tour today, dozens of well-wishers would
hasten to tell him, "You ought to write all this down and send it
in." Undoubtedly he heard the same advice in 1833. And Colonel
Thomas McKenney, interviewing him in Philadelphia, may also
have suggested it to him. Although LeClaire spoke English (with
a French accent) he was not a trained writer, and so he turned to
John B. Patterson, a young newspaper editor, for help in getting
the narrative into manuscript form. Both men swore that the final
manuscript was a true account of what Black Hawk told them.

Doubters persisted. When Thomas Ford published his depre-
cating statement many years later, Patterson was publisher of an
Illinois newspaper, the *Oquawka Spectator*. A short time after the
Ford history appeared, Patterson attacked it in the pages of the
Spectator. He called the autobiography a literal translation of
Black Hawk's own statements and said he wondered if Ford had
ever seen a copy of the book.[44]

Since there are no known documents by which the authenticity
of the work can be established, except the signed statements of
LeClaire and Patterson, much depends upon an evaluation of
those men.

Ford's statement that LeClaire was a halfbreed is true; but the
implication that he was therefore untrustworthy or incompetent
is belied by LeClaire's record. He was born in 1797, the son of a
French-Canadian father and a Potawatomi mother. Under the
sponsorship of William Clark he learned English and, allegedly,

Docket 83, 1953, before the Indian Claims Commission. Copy in the Illinois
State Historical Library. Cited hereafter as ICC.
[44] Issue of Jan. 23, 1855.

more than a dozen Indian languages, and in 1818 he was employed at Fort Armstrong as an interpreter. He served in this capacity for many years, became well known to every Indian in the area, and signed his name as interpreter to eleven treaties. In the vital treaty of September, 1832, at the close of the Black Hawk War, the Indians insisted that LeClaire be given two sections of land as a reward for faithful service. To this request General Scott replied, "It is with much pleasure that we agree to the reservation for the benefit of your faithful Interpreter. We believe that he has been faithful to both sides, to the Americans as well as to the Sac and Fox nation." [45]

LeClaire prospered with his land and with his trading business; at one time in later life he was worth half a million dollars. He was one of the founders of Davenport, Iowa, and his portrait appeared on the first five-dollar bill, authorized in 1858, for issuance by the Iowa State Bank.[46]

Patterson, born in 1806, had come to the frontier from Virginia in 1832 to visit relatives. When the war with Black Hawk began, and the publisher of the Galena newspaper, the *Galenian*, went off to join the troops, Patterson took charge. He was sworn into service as a militiaman but not as a combatant; he was detailed as regimental printer to Colonel James Strode's regiment. After the war he traded with the Indians, opened a retail store in Oquawka (south of Rock Island in Henderson County), and finally began his own newspaper in 1848. With his son, E. N. H. Patterson, he published the *Spectator* for more than forty years.[47]

In phrasing Black Hawk's story, young Patterson no doubt felt that he was conforming to the best traditions of frontier journalism. Simplicity of style had not yet become a desirable attribute in the newspaper world; a noble Indian deserved noble prose. As

[45] Minutes of the first conference held between U. S. representatives and the Indians at Rock Island, Sept. 19, 1832. Records of the U. S. Senate, 22nd Cong., NA. Seen in ICC as Petitioners' Exhibit 254.

[46] LeClaire was a tremendous man, reportedly weighing 385 pounds in 1844, but his size did not seem to hinder his movement about the country on horseback or in carriages. Most of the biographical data about him in the above paragraphs is from Snyder, 79–117.

[47] See an account of Patterson's life in *History of Mercer and Henderson Counties* (Chicago, 1882, p. 922).

a result we find Black Hawk talking of "the vicissitudes of war," and using such poetic words as "whilst," "thither," and "o'er." Patterson emphasized awkwardly humorous passages with exclamation marks. He retained certain Indian terms for a picturesque touch, and so we find Black Hawk referring to President Jackson's "wigwam," and calling newspaper editors "village criers."

To evaluate the autobiography properly we must take care to distinguish between *accuracy* and *authenticity*. The accuracy we may test by checking with contemporary documents; the authenticity — the genuineness of the book as an utterance of Black Hawk — is harder to determine.

There are inaccuracies throughout the book, but they are not basic. If Black Hawk dictated the story, the errors may be attributed to his understandable bias, his failing memory, and the involved procedure by which his words reached the printed page. Under these circumstances it is surprising that the book is so accurate.

But now we must ponder the matter of authenticity. Both LeClaire and Patterson declared, in the 1833 edition, that the book was a true record. Patterson reaffirmed this in his blast at Ford and again in the appendix to his 1882 edition. When he reissued the book in 1882, nearly fifty years after its original publication, Patterson wrote on p. 178: "After we had finished his autobiography the interpreter read it over to him carefully, and explained it thoroughly, so that he might make any needed corrections, by adding to, or taking from the narrations; but he did not desire to change it in any material manner."

Judge James Hall, writing in *History of the Indian Tribes* a few years after the autobiography appeared, said he knew that Black Hawk had acknowledged it as authentic. Hall was a reputable writer who had met and talked with Black Hawk, was acquainted with LeClaire and probably Patterson, and had no reason to misrepresent the situation.

If we wish to doubt the validity of the work, there is a document which could provide a foundation for our suspicions. The files of the Illinois State Historical Library contain a report by Major

John Dement, written after the war, giving his own account of the
battle at Kellogg's Grove. On the last page is a note by Dement,
dated December 16, 1833, saying, "The account here with for-
warded is a copy on [of] an account furnished the publisher of
Black Hawk's Biography." This tells us little, for if Patterson
had wished to concoct an account of the war he could have turned
to the files of his own *Galenian*, where most of the action was reported in detail. There is nothing in Black Hawk's account to
show that it is based on Dement's.

The text of Black Hawk's story as it appears in the following
pages is a literal reprint of the 1833 edition. If we had only this
edition and its subsequent reissues to consider, and if we could
develop nothing more questionable than Major Dement's note,
we could feel rather safe about the authenticity of the autobiography. But we must also deal with the 1882 edition.

When Patterson, as an old man, published his revised edition
of the book, he made substantial changes in the wording of many
passages and he introduced new material — attributing it to Black
Hawk. The differing language of the two editions shows that Patterson succeeded in making Black Hawk sound even less aboriginal
in 1882 then he had in 1833. Here are some typical changes:

1833 edition	*1882 edition*
. . . by the annihilation, if possi-ble, of all their race.	. . . by the utter annihilation, if possible, of the last remnant of their tribe.
He gave us a variety of presents, and plenty of provisions.	He gave us a great variety of presents, and an abundance of provisions.
I paid several visits to fort Armstrong during the summer, and was always well treated.	I paid several visits to Fort Armstrong at Rock Island, during the summer, and was always well received by the gentlemanly officers stationed there, who were distinguished for their bravery, and they never trampled upon an enemy's rights.

These are unimportant changes from the standpoint of accuracy, though the last one casts doubt upon Patterson's claim that

the book is a "literal translation" of Black Hawk's words. They are not nearly as significant as the completely new portions that Patterson added. The new material includes (1) a tale about Elijah Kilbourn, allegedly captured by Black Hawk and forced to live with the Sauk for three years, then recaptured during the Black Hawk War; (2) a paragraph about Black Hawk's "watch tower" on the Mississippi; (3) a legend about a pair of Indian lovers buried beneath a rock slide; (4) a passage about the persons who accompanied Black Hawk on his trip to the East, containing errors of fact; (5) a verbatim account of a speech made in honor of Black Hawk by John A. Graham, in New York.

In weaving this new material into the text, Patterson made no attempt to indicate that it was new or that it was never related by Black Hawk. When referring to the Kilbourn affair in his commentary on the war, p. 158, he said, "Mr. K. is the man Black Hawk *makes mention of* in his narrative as having been taken captive during our last war with Great Britain, and by him adopted into the Sac tribe; and again taken prisoner by three of his braves at the battle of Sycamore creek." [Italics added.]

If Patterson altered Black Hawk's story in the 1882 edition, must we assume that he did so forty-nine years earlier in the 1833 edition? Not necessarily. The Patterson of 1882, to whom the Black Hawk period was a fading memory, certainly must have viewed the book differently than he had as a young printer working closely with LeClaire and Black Hawk. He was probably more concerned in 1882 with telling a story than with preserving a document of American history; and his two associates were not there to confirm or deny. If we are to evaluate Black Hawk's story properly, we must disregard the 1882 edition and stick with the 1833 edition, which, despite the intrusive hands of interpreter and editor, is basically a tale told by an Indian from an Indian point of view.

Like much Americana, it is a tragic tale, for tragedy and inequity are certain in the re-peopling of a continent. Black Hawk's seventy-year lifetime was one of struggle and change—from his early battles with the Osage to his last miserable flight before an American army. He saw Spanish rule give way to American rule, and the westward press of settlers that resulted. He saw America and Great

Britain involved in a disgraceful war, and he fought on the British side until he grew tired of it. When he drew his mark on the white man's treaty papers, it was always with the fear that the covenants would not hold.

Black Hawk was never a great Indian statesman like Tecumseh or a persuasive orator like Keokuk. He was not a hereditary chief or a medicine man. He was only a stubborn warrior brooding upon the certainty that his people must fight to survive.

The Indians used to say that a white settlement was like a spot of raccoon grease on a new blanket. When you first saw the tiny stain you did not realize how wide and how fast it would spread. Black Hawk's story is the narrative of a man who saw the vast stain of American settlement widening across the Midwest, darkening all the lands of his ancestors. Keokuk was a smooth talker and a politician who planned to co-exist with the Americans; Black Hawk was a bull-headed fighter who chose a bitter last stand against extinction. And both men went down, for their day in history had passed.

LIFE

OF

MA-KA-TAI-ME-SHE-KIA-KIAK

OR

BLACK HAWK,

EMBRACING THE

TRADITION OF HIS NATION—INDIAN WARS IN WHICH HE HAS
BEEN ENGAGED—CAUSE OF JOINING THE BRITISH IN THEIR
LATE WAR WITH AMERICA, AND ITS HISTORY—DES-
CRIPTION OF THE ROCK-RIVER VILLAGE—MAN-
NERS AND CUSTOMS—ENCROACHMENTS BY
THE WHITES, CONTRARY TO TREATY—
REMOVAL FROM HIS VILLAGE IN 1831.

WITH AN ACCOUNT OF THE CAUSE

AND

GENERAL HISTORY

OF THE

LATE WAR,

HIS SURRENDER AND CONFINEMENT AT JEFFERSON BARRACKS,

AND

TRAVELS THROUGH THE UNITED STATES.

DICTATED BY HIMSELF.

CINCINNATI:

1833.

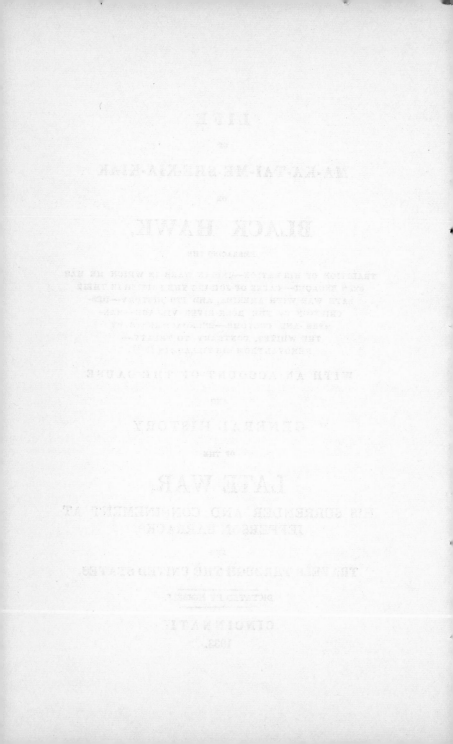

INDIAN AGENCY, Rock-Island, *October* 16, 1833.

I DO HEREBY CERTIFY, that Mà-ka-tai-me-she-kià-kiàk, or Black Hawk, did call upon me, on his return to his people in August last, and express a great desire to have a History of his Life written and published, in order, (as he said) "that the people of the United States, (among whom he had been travelling, and by whom he had been treated with great respect, friendship and hospitality,) might know the *causes* that had impelled him to act as he has done, and the *principles* by which he was governed." In accordance with his request, I acted as Interpreter; and was particularly cautious, to understand distinctly the narrative of Black Hawk throughout — and have examined the work carefully, since its completion — and have no hesitation in pronouncing it strictly correct, in all its particulars.

Given under my hand, at the Sac and Fox Agency, the day and date above written.

ANTOINE LeCLAIR,
U. S. Interpreter for the Sacs and Foxes.

MA-NE-SE-NO OKE-MAUT WAP-PI MA-QUAI.

WA-TA-SAI WE-YEU,

Ai nan-ni ta co-si-ya-quai, na-katch ai she-ke she-he-nack, hai-me-ka-ti ya-quai ke-she-he-nack, ken-e-cha we-he-ke kai-pec-kien a-cob, ai we-ne-she we-he-yen; ne-wai-ta-sa-mak ke-kosh-pe kai-a-poi qui-wat. No-ta-wach-pai pai-ke se-na-mon nan-ni-yoo, ai-ke-kai na-o-pen. Ni-me-to sai-ne-ni-wen, ne-ta-to-ta ken ai mo-he-man tà-ta-que, ne-me-to-sai-ne-ne-wen.

Nin-à-kài-ka poi-pon-ni chi-cha-yen, kai-kà-ya ha-ma-we pa-she-to-he-yen. Kài-nà-ya kai-nen-ne-naip, he-nok ki-nok ke-chà-kai-ya, pai-no-yen ne-ket-te-sim-mak o-ke-te-wak ke-o-che, me-ka ti-ya-quois na-kach mai-quoi, à-que-qui pà-che-qui ke-kan-ni tà-men-nin. Ke-to-tà we-yen, à-que-kà-ni-co-te she-tai-hai yen-nen, chai-chà-me-co kai-ke-me-se ai we-ke ken-ne-tà-mo-wàt, ken-na-wà-ha-o mà-co-quà-yeai-quoi. Ken-wen-na àk-che-màn wen-ni-ta-hài ke-men-ne to-tà-we-yeu, ke-kog-hài ke-ta-shi ke-kài-nà-we-yen, he-na-cha wài-che-we to-mo-nan, ai pe-che-quà-chi mo-pen mà-me-co, mài-che-we-tà nà-mo-nan, ne-ya-we-nan qui-a-hà-wa pe-ta-kek, a-que-yeàr tak-pa-she-qui à-to-tà-mo-wat, chi-ye-tuk he-ne cha-wài-chi he-ni-nan ke-o-chi-tà mow-tà-swee-pài che-quà-que.

He-ni-cha-hài poi-kài-nen nà-na-so-si-yen, ai o-sà-ke-we-yen, ke-pe-me-kai-mi-kat hài-nen hac-yái na-na-co-si-peu, nen-à-kài-ne-co-ten ne-co-ten ne-ka chi-a-quoi ne-me-cok me-to-sai ne-ne.wak-kài ne-we-yen-nen, kài-shài mà-ni-to· ke ka-to-me-nak ke-wa-sài he-co-wai mi-à-me· kà-chi pài-ko-tài-hear-pe kài-cee wà-wà-kià he-pe hà-pe-nach-he-chà, na-na-ke.nà-way ni-taain ai we-pa-he-weà to-to-nà cà, ke-to-ta-we-yeak, he-nok mià-ni ai she-ke-tà ma-ke-si-yen, nen-a-kai nà-co-ten ne-ka-he-nen é-ta-quois, wà-toi-na-ka che-mà-ke-keu nà-ta-che tài-hài-ken ai mo-co-man ye-we-yeu ke-to-towé. E-nok mà-ni-hài she-ka-tà-ma ka-si-yen, wen-e-cha-hài nài-ne-mak, mài-ko-ten ke-kà-cha mà-men-na-tuk we-yowé, keu-ke-nok ai she-me ma-nà-ni tà-men-ke-yowé.

MA-KA-TAI-ME-SHE-KIA-KIAK.

Ma-tàus-we Ki-sis, 1833.

[TRANSLATION.]

DEDICATION.

TO BRIGADIER GEN'L. H. ATKINSON.

SIR, — The changes of fortune, and vicissitudes of war, made you my conqueror. When my last resources were exhausted, my warriors worn down with long and toilsome marches, we yielded, and I became your prisoner.

The story of my life is told in the following pages; it is intimately connected, and in some measure, identified with a part of the history of your own: I have, therefore, dedicated it to you.

The changes of many summers, have brought old age upon me,— and I cannot expect to survive many moons. Before I set out on my journey to the land of my fathers, I have determined to give my motives and reasons for my former hostilities to the whites, and to vindicate my character from misrepresentation. The kindness I received from you whilst a prisoner of war, assures me that you will vouch for the facts contained in my narrative, so far as they came under your observation.

I am now an obscure member of a nation, that formerly honored and respected my opinions. The path to glory is rough, and many gloomy hours obscure it. May the Great Spirit shed light on your's — and that you may never experience the humility that the power of the American government has reduced me to, is the wish of him, who, in his native forests, was once as proud and bold as yourself.

BLACK HAWK.

10th Moon, 1833.

ADVERTISEMENT.

IT is presumed no apology will be required for presenting to the
public, the life of a Hero who has lately taken such high rank
among the distinguished individuals of America. In the following
pages he will be seen in the characters of a Warrior, a Patriot and
a State-prisoner — in every situation he is still the Chief of his
Band, asserting their rights with dignity, firmness and courage.
Several accounts of the late war having been published, in which
he thinks justice is not done to himself or nation, he determined
to make known to the world, the injuries his people have received
from the whites — the causes which brought on the war on the part
of his nation, and a general history of it throughout the campaign.
In his opinion, this is the only method now left him, to rescue his
little Band — the remnant of those who fought bravely with him —
from the effects of the statements that have already gone forth.

   The facts which he states, respecting the Treaty of 1804, in vir-
tue of the provisions of which Government claimed the country
in dispute, and enforced its arguments with the sword, are worthy
of attention. It purported to cede to the United States, all the
country, including the village and corn fields of Black Hawk and
his band, on the east side of the Mississippi. Four individuals of
the tribe, who were on a visit to St. Louis to obtain the liberation

of one of their people from prison, were prevailed upon, (says Black Hawk,) to make this important treaty, without the knowledge or authority of the tribes, or nation.

In treating with the Indians for their country, it has always been customary to assemble the whole nation; because, as has been truly suggested by the Secretary of War, the nature of the authority of the chiefs of a tribe is such, that it is not often that they dare make a treaty of much consequence, — and we might add, never, when involving so much magnitude as the one under consideration, without the presence of their young men. A rule so reasonable and just ought never to be violated — and the Indians might well question the right of Government to dispossess them, when such violation was made the basis of its right.

The Editor has written this work according to the dictation of Black Hawk, through the United States' Interpreter, at the Sac and Fox Agency of Rock Island. He does not, therefore, consider himself responsible for any of the facts, or views, contained in it — and leaves the old Chief and his story with the public, whilst he neither asks, nor expects, any fame for his services as an amanuensis.

THE EDITOR.

WISCONSIN

IOWA

Mississippi River

Illinois River

ILLINOIS

Extent of the land cession in the Treaty of 1804. Based on Royce.

MISSOURI

life of black hawk

I was born at the Sac Village,[1] on Rock river, in the year 1767, and am now in my 67th year. My great grand father, Na-nà-ma-kee, or Thunder, (according to the tradition given me by my father, Py-e-sa,) was born in the vicinity of Montreal, where the Great Spirit first placed the Sac Nation,[2] and inspired him with a belief that, at the end of four years, he should see a *white man*, who would be to him a father. Consequently he blacked his face, and eat but once a day, (just as the sun was going down,) for three years, and continued dreaming throughout all this time whenever he slept — when the Great Spirit again appeared to him, and told him, that, at the end of one year more, he should meet his father, — and directed him to start seven days before its expiration, and take with him his two brothers *Na-mah*, or Sturgeon, and *Pau-ka-hum-ma-wa* or Sun Fish, and travel in a direction to the left of sun-rising. After

[1] Saukenuk, a large and permanent Sauk village on the Rock River, a short distance above its confluence with the Mississippi. It was probably burned in 1780 by George Rogers Clark, and was burned again by Illinois militiamen in 1831. A residential section of Rock Island, Illinois, is now built upon the site of the old village.

[2] Throughout Black Hawk's story his people are called Sacs, but the name has had many variations. The Indians called themselves Saukies, and contemporary documents refer to them as Sockeys, Socks, Sacques, Sackies, Saucs, etc. They have generally come to be called the Sauk. (The accepted practice today is to use the singular form for tribal names.)

pursuing this course five days, he sent out his two brothers to listen if they could hear a noise, and if so, to fasten some grass to the end of a pole, erect it, pointing in the direction of the sound, and then return to him.

Early next morning they returned, and reported that they had heard sounds which appeared near at hand, and that they had fulfilled his order. They all then started for the place where the pole had been erected; when, on reaching it, Na-nà-ma-kee left his party, and went alone to the place from whence the sounds proceeded, and found that the white man [3] had arrived and pitched his tent. When he came in sight, his father [4] came out to meet him. He took him by the hand, and welcomed him into his tent. He told him that he was the son of the King of France — that he had been dreaming for four years — that the Great Spirit had directed him to come here, where he should meet a nation of people who had never yet seen a white man — that they should be his children, and he should be their father — that he had communicated these things to the King, his father, who laughed at him, and called him a Ma-she-na — but he insisted on coming here to meet his children, where the Great Spirit had directed him. The King told him that he would neither find land nor people — that this was an uninhabited region of lakes and mountains; but, finding that he would have no peace without it, fitted out a nà-pe-quâ, manned it, and gave it to him in charge, when he immediately loaded it, set sail, and had now landed on the very day that the Great Spirit had told him, in his dreams, he should meet his children. He had now met the man who should, in future, have charge of all the nation.

He then presented him with a medal,[5] which he hung round his

---

[3] This tradition may be based upon the visits of Champlain, the French explorer who first visited Canada in 1603 and later brought colonists to the site of Quebec.

[4] The Indians used the father-son terminology to indicate their relationship to officials of European governments. When Black Hawk speaks of visiting his British father at Mackinac or Malden he means the commander of the British fort at one of those places. And later he calls the President of the United States his Great Father.

[5] Black Hawk's frequent mention of medals is evidence of the importance that he and every Indian attached to them. Medals were so valuable as symbols of rank and authority that they had become a part of tribal legends. Each Euro-

neck. Na-nà-ma-kee informed him of *his* dreaming, — and told him that his two brothers remained a little ways behind. His father gave him a shirt, blanket, and handkerchief, besides a variety of presents, and told him to go and bring his brothers. Having laid aside his buffalo robe, and dressed himself in his new dress, he started to meet his brethren. When they met, he explained to them his meeting with the white man, and exhibited to their view the presents that he had made him — took off his medal, and placed it upon Nàh-ma, his elder brother, and requested them both to go with him to his father. They proceeded thither, — were ushered into the tent, and after some brief ceremony, his father opened his chest and took presents therefrom for the new-comers. He discovered that Na-nà-ma-kee had given his medal to Nàh-ma. He told him that he had done wrong — he should wear that medal himself, as he had others for his brethren: That which he had given him was a type of the rank he should hold in the nation: That his brothers could only rank as *civil* chiefs, — and their duties should consist of taking care of the village, and attending to its civil concerns — whilst his rank, from his superior knowledge, placed him over them all. If the nation gets into any difficulty with another, then his puc-co-hà-wà-ma, or sovereign decree, must be obeyed. If he declared war, he must lead them on to battle: That the Great Spirit had made him a great and brave general, and had sent him here to give him that medal, and make presents to him for his people.

His father remained four days — during which time he gave him guns, powder and lead, spears and lances, and showed him their use — so that in war he could chastise his enemies, — and in peace they could kill buffalo, deer and other game, necessary for the comforts and luxuries of life. He then presented the others with

pean nation, when assuming jurisdiction of a tribe, was anxious to recover all existing medals and replace them with new issues. The Sauk and Fox were among the tribes receiving medals at a large council at Montreal in 1778. After the War of 1812, Britain struck a special silver medal to mark its appreciation for the military service of her Indian allies.

During Jefferson's administration the United States adopted a series of peace medals, each bearing on the obverse the image of a President. For a general discussion of Indian medals, see the article by P. E. Beckwith in Hodge, I, 829–36.

various kinds of cooking utensils, and learned them their uses, — and having given them a large quantity of goods, as presents, and every other thing necessary for their comfort, he set sail for France, after promising to meet them again, at the same place after the twelfth moon.

The three newly-made chiefs returned to their village, and explained to Muk-a-tà-quet, their father, who was the principal chief of the nation, what had been said and done. The old chief had some *dogs* killed, and made a feast, preparatory to resigning his sceptre, to which all the nation were invited. Great anxiety prevailed among them, to know what the three brothers had seen and heard, — when the old chief rose, and related to them the sayings and doings of his three sons; and concluded by observing, that "the Great Spirit had directed that these, his three children, should take the rank and power that had been his, — and that he yielded these honors and duties willingly to them, — because it was the wish of the Great Spirit, and he could never consent to make him angry!" He now presented the great medicine bag to Na-nà-ma-kee, and told him, "that he cheerfully resigned it to him — it is the soul of our nation — it has never yet been disgraced — and I will expect you to keep it unsullied!"

Some dissension arose among some of them, in consequence of so much power being given to Na-nà-ma-kee, he being so young a man. To quiet this, Na-nà-ma-kee, during a violent *thunder storm*, told them that he had *caused* it! and that it was an exemplification of the *name* the Great Spirit had given him. During this storm, the *lightning* struck, and set fire to, a tree, close by; (a sight they had never witnessed before.) He went to it, and brought away some of its burning branches, made a fire in the lodge, and seated his brothers thereby, opposite to each other; whilst he stood up, and addressed his people as follows:

"I am yet young — but the Great Spirit has called me to the rank I now hold among you. I have never sought to be any thing more than my birth entitled me. I have not been ambitious — nor was it ever my wish, whilst my father lives, to have taken his place — nor have I now usurped his powers. The Great Spirit caused me to dream for four years, — he told me where to go and meet the white man, who would be a kind father to us all. I obeyed his order. I went, and have seen our new father. You have all heard what was said and done. The Great Spirit directed him to come and meet me, and it is his order that places me at the head of my nation,— the place which my father has willingly resigned.

"You have all witnessed the power which has been given to me by the Great Spirit, in making that fire — and all that I now ask is, that these, my two chiefs, may never let it go out: That they preserve peace among you, and administer to the wants of the needy: And, should an enemy invade our country, I will then, but not until then, assume command, and go forth with my band of brave warriors, and endeavor to chastise them!"

At the conclusion of this speech, every voice cried out for Na-nà-ma-kee! All were satisfied, when they found that the *Great Spirit had done*, what they had suspected was the work of Na-nà-ma-kee, he being a very shrewd young man.

The next spring, according to promise, their French father returned, with his nà-pe-quâ richly laden with goods, which were distributed among them. He continued for a long time to keep up a regular trade with them — they giving him in exchange for his goods, furs and peltries.

After a long time the British overpowered the French, (the two nations being at war,) drove them away from Quebec, and took possession of it themselves.[6] The different tribes of Indians around our nation, envying our people, united their forces against them, and succeeded, by their great strength, to drive them to Montreal, and from thence to Mackinac.

Here our people first met our British father, who furnished them with goods. Their enemies still pursued them, and drove them to different places on the lake, until they made a village near Green Bay, on what is now called *Sac* river,[7] having derived its name from

[6] Sir David Kirke, English adventurer and merchant, forced Champlain to surrender Quebec in 1629. It was restored to the French three years later because Charles I had made peace with France, and was not held again by the British until Gen. James Wolfe captured it in 1759. Since Black Hawk's narrative does not mention the restoration of Quebec to the French, it may be that the Sauk were driven away during 1629–32 while the British were in possession.
[7] The Fox River.

this circumstance. Here they held a council with the Foxes, and a national treaty of friendship and alliance was concluded upon. The Foxes abandoned their village, and joined the Sacs. This arrangement being mutually obligatory upon both parties, as neither were sufficiently strong to meet their enemies with any hope of success, they soon became as one band or nation of people. They were driven, however, by the combined forces of their enemies, to the Wisconsin. They remained here some time, until a party of their young men, (who had descended Rock river to its mouth,) returned, and made a favorable report of the country. They all descended Rock river — drove the Kas-kas-kias from the country, and commenced the erection of their village, determined never to leave it.[8]

At this village I was born, being a regular descendant of the first chief, Na-nà-ma-kee, or Thunder. Few, if any, events of note, transpired within my recollection, until about my fifteenth year. I was not allowed to paint, or wear feathers; but distinguished myself, at that early age, by wounding an enemy; consequently, I was placed in the ranks of the Braves!

Soon after this, a leading chief of the Muscow[9] nation, came to our village for recruits to go to war against the Osages,[10] our com-

[8] This is a sketchy but basically accurate account of Sauk and Fox history as we know it. The Sauk and Fox are of Algonquian stock. Their wanderings took them into the Saginaw Bay region of eastern Michigan, and "Saginaw" means "country of the Sauk." By 1667 the two tribes were living around Green Bay in northeast Wisconsin. After the French had reduced the Fox to a defenseless fraction of their former strength, about 1730, the two tribes became allied. The French called the Fox the "Renards," and they are designated as Reynards in many territorial documents. They call themselves the Mesquakie. In 1805 Lewis and Clark estimated the Sauk population at 2,000 and the Fox population at 1,200. Most of the brief descriptions of Indian tribes in the notes that follow are based on Swanton, *The Indian Tribes of North America*.
[9] Probably the Mascouten nation.
[10] A Siouan tribe related by language to the Omaha, Ponca, Kansa, and Quapaw. There were three divisions, the Big Osage living on the Osage River in Missouri, the Little Osage on the Missouri River, and a third band on the Arkansas River. The Osage were famous as fighters among the southern Plains tribes and were usually warring with their neighbors. Lewis and Clark estimated about 1,400 warriors in the combined bands in 1805. (See Swanton, 271–73.) The Sauk and Fox once sent 1,000 warriors against them in a single party. (Esarey, ed., *Messages and Letters of William Henry Harrison*, cited hereafter as *Harrison's Messages and Letters*.)

mon enemy. I volunteered my services to go, as my father had joined him; and was proud to have an opportunity to prove to him that I was not an unworthy son, and that I had courage and bravery. It was not long before we met the enemy, when a battle immediately ensued. Standing by my father's side, I saw him kill his antagonist, and tear the scalp from his head. Fired with valor and ambition, I rushed furiously upon another, smote him to the earth with my tomahawk — run my lance through his body — took off his scalp, and returned in triumph to my father! He said nothing, but looked pleased. This was the first man I killed! The enemy's loss in this engagement having been great, they immediately retreated, which put an end to the war for the present. Our party then returned to our village, and danced over the scalps we had taken. This was the first time that I was permitted to join in a scalp-dance.

After a few moons had passed, (having acquired considerable fame as a *brave*,) I led a party of seven, and attacked *one hundred Osages!* I killed one man, and left him for my comrades to scalp, whilst I was taking an observation of the strength and preparations of the enemy; and finding that they were all equally well armed with ourselves, I ordered a retreat, and came off without losing a man! This excursion gained for me great applause, and enabled me, before a great while, to raise a party of one hundred and eighty, to go against the Osages. We left our village in high spirits, and marched over a rugged country, until we reached that of the Osages, on the Missouri. We followed their trail until we arrived at their village, which we approached with great caution, expecting that they were all there; but found, to our sorrow, that they had deserted it! The party became dissatisfied, in consequence of this disappointment, — and all, with the exception of *five*, dispersed and returned home. I then placed myself at the head of this brave little band, and thanked the Great Spirit that *so many* remained, — and took up the trail of our enemies, with a full determination never to return without some trophy of victory! We followed on for several days — killed one man and a boy, and then returned with their scalps.

In consequence of this mutiny in my camp, I was not again enabled to raise a sufficient party to go against the Osages, until about my nineteenth year. During this interim, they committed many outrages on our nation and people. I succeeded at length, in recruiting two hundred efficient warriors, and took up the line of march early in the morning. In a few days we were in the enemy's country, and had not travelled far before we met an equal force to contend with. A general battle immediately commenced, although my braves were considerably fatigued by forced marches. Each party fought desperately. The enemy seemed unwilling to yield the ground, and we were determined to conquer or die! A large number of the Osages were killed, and many wounded, before they commenced retreating. A band of warriors more brave, skilful, and efficient than mine, could not be found. In this engagement I killed five men and one squaw, and had the good fortune to take the scalps of all I struck, except one. The enemy's loss in this engagement was about one hundred men. Ours nineteen. We now returned to our village, well pleased with our success, and danced over the scalps we had taken.

The Osages, in consequence of their great loss in this battle, became satisfied to remain on their own lands; and ceased, for awhile, their depredations on our nation. Our attention, therefore, was directed towards an ancient enemy, who had decoyed and murdered some of our helpless women and children. I started, with my father, who took command of a small party, and proceeded against the enemy. We met near Merimack,[11] and an action ensued; the Cherokees[12] having greatly the advantage in numbers. Early in this engagement my father was wounded in the thigh — but had the pleasure of killing his antagonist before he fell. Seeing that he had fallen, I assumed command, and fought desperately, until the enemy commenced retreating before us. I returned to my father to administer to his necessities, but nothing could be done for him. The *medicine man* said the wound was *mortal!* from which he soon

[11] The Meramec River in Missouri, flowing into the Mississippi River a few miles below St. Louis.

[12] An Iroquoian tribe centered in the higher areas at the southern end of the Appalachians, particularly Tennessee and North Carolina. In 1838, when they were forcibly removed to the West by the American government, their population was estimated at 22,500.

after *died!* In this battle I killed three men, and wounded several. The enemy's loss being twenty-eight, and ours seven.

I now fell heir to the great *medicine bag* [13] of my forefathers, which had belonged to my father. I took it, buried our dead, and returned with my party, all sad and sorrowful, to our village, in consequence of the loss of my father. Owing to this misfortune, I blacked my face, fasted, and prayed to the Great Spirit for five years — during which time I remained in a civil capacity, hunting and fishing. [14]

The Osages having commenced aggressions on our people, and the Great Spirit having taken pity on me, I took a small party and went against the enemy, but could only find *six* men! Their forces being so weak, I thought it cowardly to kill them, — but took them prisoners, and carried them to our Spanish father [15] at St. Louis, and gave them up to him; and then returned to our village. Determined on the final extermination of the Osages, for the injuries our nation and people had received from them, I commenced recruiting a strong force, immediately on my return, and started, in the third moon, with five hundred Sacs and Foxes, and one hundred Ioways, [16] and marched against the enemy. We continued our march for several days before we came upon their trail, which was discovered late in the day. We encamped for the night; made an early start next morning, and before sun down, fell upon *forty lodges*, and killed all their inhabitants, except *two squaws!* whom I captured and made prisoners. During this attack I killed seven men and two boys, with my own hand.

[13] A bundle made of skins, fabric, or birch bark, containing a collection of charms and amulets associated with the religious life of the Indians. A bundle might contain such magical objects as a bag of cedar leaves, a braid of sweetgrass, a buffalo tail amulet, a hawk skin, etc. (See Harrington.)
[14] Usually a Sauk mourned the loss of close relations from six months to a year. He blackened his face, neglected his personal appearance, and remained comparatively inactive. A woman mourned the loss of a husband at least a year, then resumed her normal paint and costume and went searching for another husband. (Morse, 137–38.)
[15] Charles Dehault Delassus, who had been Spanish governor of upper Louisiana since 1799.
[16] A Siouan tribe, related by language to the Oto and Missouri Indians, and living mainly within the present boundaries of the state of Iowa. Lewis and Clark in 1804 estimated their population at 800.

In this engagement many of the bravest warriors among the Osages were killed, which caused the balance of their nation to remain on their own lands, and cease their aggressions upon our hunting grounds.

The loss of my father, by the Cherokees, made me anxious to avenge his death, by the annihilation, if possible, of all their race. I accordingly commenced recruiting another party to go against them. Having succeeded in this, I started, with my party, and went into their country, but only found five of their people, whom I took prisoners. I afterwards released four men — the other, a young *squaw*, we brought home. Great as was my hatred for this people, I could not kill so small a party.

During the close of the ninth moon, I led a large party against the Chippewas,[17] Kaskaskias [18] and Osages. This was the commencement of a long and arduous campaign, which terminated in my thirty-fifth year: Having had seven regular engagements, and a number of small skirmishes. During this campaign, several hundred of the enemy were slain. I killed *thirteen* of their bravest warriors, with my own hand.[19]

[17] The Chippewa or Ojibwa Indians, of the Algonquian language group, were first found in the region of Sault Ste Marie, but later ranged over the entire northern shore of Lake Huron and both shores of Lake Superior, the northern interior, and as far west as the Turtle Mountains of North Dakota. In the nineteenth century they were grouped into reservations on both sides of the International Boundary. Estimated population in 1843, about 30,000.

[18] An Illinois tribe, reduced in number by intertribal warfare and disease and dispossessed of their lands by the Sauk, Fox, Kickapoo, and Potawatomi tribes. In 1800 there were only about 150 left, and in 1832 the survivors moved west, first to the Kansas area and then, in 1868, to Oklahoma with the Peoria, Wea, and Piankashaw.

[19] Black Hawk is often hazy about dates, even though he probably had help from his interpreter and editor in pinning down the times of various events. If the campaign against the Osage and other tribes ended in his thirty-fifth year, as he says, this would have been about 1801 or 1802. A few years later, several tribes were induced by the American government to sign a treaty in St. Louis, agreeing to cease their traditional warfare. The tribes included the Delaware, Miami, Potawatomi, Kickapoo, Sauk, Fox, Kaskaskia, Sioux, and Osage. The treaty, signed Oct. 18, 1805, was ineffective and the Sauk were still warring with the Osage as late as 1811–12. (Carter, ed., *Territorial Papers of the United States*, 13:245, 14:271, and 14:588. Cited hereafter as *Terr. Papers*.)

The attitude of the United States changed during the War of 1812, and intertribal fighting was promoted as a matter of policy. Gov. William Clark told

Our enemies having now been driven from our hunting grounds, with so great a loss as they sustained, we returned, in peace, to our villages; and after the seasons of mourning and burying our dead relations, and of feast-dancing had passed, we commenced preparations for our winter's hunt, in which we were very successful.

We generally paid a visit to St. Louis every summer; but, in consequence of the protracted war in which we had been engaged, I had not been there for some years. Our difficulties having all been settled, I concluded to take a small party, that summer, and go down to see our Spanish father. We went — and on our arrival, put up our lodges where the market-house now stands. After painting and dressing, we called to see our Spanish father, and were well received. He gave us a variety of presents, and plenty of provisions. We danced through the town as usual, and its inhabitants all seemed to be well pleased. They appeared to us like brothers — and always gave us good advice.

On my next, and *last*, visit to my Spanish father, I discovered, on landing, that all was not right: every countenance seemed sad and gloomy! I inquired the cause, and was informed that the Americans were coming to take possession of the town and country! — and that we should then lose our Spanish father! This news made myself and band sad — because we had always heard bad accounts of the Americans from Indians who had lived near them! — and we were sorry to lose our Spanish father, who had always treated us with great friendship.

A few days afterwards, the Americans arrived.[20] I took my band,

the Secretary of War in 1814: ". . . policy obliges me to incourage the Osage and the Tribes on the Missouri to wage War on the Mississippi Indians &ᵉ Those Missouri Tribes must either be engaged for us; or they will be opposed to us without doubt." (*Terr. Papers*, 14:786.)

Thomas Forsyth, a trader and Indian agent of long experience, once said he never knew two tribes of Indians to make peace with each other except when the U. S. government interfered. Once war commenced, he said, it always led to the final extermination of one or the other of the parties. (Forsyth to Clark, Jan. 15, 1827. Draper mss., 9T12, in whi.)

[20] A detail of American soldiers, commanded by Capt. Amos Stoddard, had come on March 9, 1804, to take formal possession of the upper portion of the Louisiana Purchase. Stoddard (1762–1813) was a veteran of the Revolution and a onetime Massachusetts legislator who had been chosen to accept the Territory from Spain in the name of France, and on the following day to accept it from

and went to take leave, for the last time, of our father. The Americans came to see him also. Seeing them approach, we passed out at one door, as they entered another — and immediately started, in canoes, for our village on Rock river — not liking the change any more than our friends appeared to, at St. Louis.[21]

On arriving at our village, we gave the news, that strange people had taken St. Louis — and that we should never see our Spanish father again! This information made all our people sorry!

Some time afterwards, a boat came up the river, with a young American chief, [Lieutenant (afterwards General) Pike,][22] and a small party of soldiers. We heard of him, (by runners,) soon after he had passed Salt river. Some of our young braves watched him every day, to see what sort of people he had on board! The boat, at length, arrived at Rock river, and the young chief came on shore with his interpreter — made a speech, and gave us some presents! We, in return, presented him with meat, and such provisions as we could spare.

We were all well pleased with the speech of the young chief. He gave us good advice; said our American father would treat us well. He presented us an American flag, which was hoisted. He then requested us to pull down our *British flags* — and give him our *British medals* — promising to send us others on his return to St. Louis. This we declined, as we wished to have *two Fathers!*

When the young chief started, we sent runners to the Fox village,

France on behalf of the United States. He was then appointed civil and military governor of the territory for the first few months of its existence. He was fatally wounded during the siege of Fort Meigs during the War of 1812, a battle in which Black Hawk fought on the side of the British.

[21] The change of "fathers" aroused much interest among the Indians. Amos Stoddard wrote to William Claiborne, March 26, 1804, that he was experiencing "infinite trouble from the Indians." He said, "They crowd here by the hundreds to see their new father, and to hear his words." Within a few months Stoddard had discovered that the Sauk were not in a hurry to shift their loyalty from Spain to America. Writing to Henry Dearborn, June 3, he complained, "The Saucks . . . certainly do not pay that respect to the United States which is entertained by the other Indians — and in some instances they have assumed a pretty elevated tone." (Mo. Hist. Soc., *Glimpses of the Past*, 2 (1933-35) 98, 111.)

[22] All bracketed words in the text were inserted by J. B. Patterson, the original editor.

some miles distant, to direct them to treat him well as he passed — which they did. He went to the head of the Mississippi, and then returned to St. Louis. We did not see any Americans again for some time, — being supplied with goods by British traders.

We were fortunate in not giving up our medals — for we learned afterwards, from our traders, that the chiefs high up on the Mississippi, who gave theirs, never received any in exchange for them. But the fault was not with the young American chief. He was a good man, and a great brave — and died in his country's service.[23]

Some moons after this young chief descended the Mississippi, one of our people killed an American — and was confined, in the prison at St. Louis, for the offence. We held a council at our village to see what could be done for him, — which determined that Quàsh-quà-me, Pà-she-pa-ho, Oú-che-quà-ka, and Hà-she-quar-hi-qua, should go down to St. Louis, see our American father, and do all they could to have our friend released: by paying for the person killed — thus covering the blood, and satisfying the relations of the man murdered! This being the only means with us of saving a person who had killed another — and we *then* thought it was the same way with the whites!

The party started with the good wishes of the whole nation — hoping they would accomplish the object of their mission. The relatives of the prisoner blacked their faces, and fasted — hoping the Great Spirit would take pity on them, and return the husband and father to his wife and children.

Quàsh-quà-me and party remained a long time absent. They at length returned, and encamped a short distance below the village — but did not come up that day — nor did any person approach their camp! They appeared to be dressed in *fine coats*, and had *medals!* From these circumstances, we were in hopes that they had brought good news. Early the next morning, the Council Lodge was crowded — Quàsh-quà-me and party came up, and gave us the following account of their mission:

[23] Zebulon Montgomery Pike (1779–1813) related his encounter with the Sauk and Fox in his journal (Coues, ed., 15–18). Pike was leading an exploring party, in 1805, to find the source of the Mississippi. He was later killed during the War of 1812.

"On their arrival at St. Louis, they met their American father,[24] and explained to him their business, and urged the release of their friend. The American chief told them he wanted land — and they had agreed to give him some on the west side of the Mississippi, and some on the Illinois side opposite the Jeffreon. When the business was all arranged, they expected to have their friend released to come home with them. But about the time they were ready to start, their friend was let out of prison, who ran a short distance, and was *shot dead!*[25] This is all they could recollect of what was said and done. They had been drunk the greater part of the time they were in St. Louis."

This is all myself or nation knew of the treaty of 1804. It has been explained to me since. I find, by that treaty, all our country, east of the Mississippi, and south of the Jeffreon, was ceded to the United States for *one thousand dollars* a year! I will leave it to the people of the United States to say, whether our nation was properly represented in this treaty? or whether we received a fair compensation for the extent of country ceded by those *four* individuals? I could say much about this treaty, but I will not, at this time. It has been the origin of all our difficulties.[26]

[24] William Henry Harrison (1773–1841) had been named by Jefferson as a special official to deal with the Indians on the subject of land cessions and boundary lines. He served as governor of the Indiana Territory, and for a few months as governor of the Louisiana Territory.

[25] The young chief was not already confined at St. Louis, as Black Hawk says, but was taken there by the Sauk to give himself up as a peace offering. He had been involved in the killing of three settlers at the Cuivre (Quiver) River settlement north of St. Louis. When it later developed that he had killed in self-defense, President Jefferson sent a letter of pardon for him. But the letter came too late; he had already escaped from the guard house, according to Governor Harrison's account, and had been killed by a sentinel. (*Harrison's Messages and Letters*, I, 132–34.)

The murder of the settlers occurred more than a year before Pike's expedition, not after it as Black Hawk says.

[26] Much confusion surrounds the treaty of 1804, the text of which is on p. 157, below. It is true that the Sauk and Fox had asked, as early as 1802, for a treaty which would give them an annuity. (*Harrison's Messages and Letters*, I, 44.) But at that time they were only familiar with the British practice of giving annuities as gifts, without land cession or other consideration in return.

Harrison had been authorized by the government to enter into a treaty with the Sauk and Fox. The Indians had been notified that they were to send some

Some time after this treaty was made, a war chief, with a party of soldiers, came up in keel boats, and encamped a short distance above the head of the Des Moines rapids, and commenced cutting timber and building houses. The news of their arrival was soon carried to all the villages — when council after council was held. We could not understand the intention, or reason, why the Americans wanted to build houses at that place — but were told that they were a party of soldiers, who had brought *great guns* with them — and looked like a *war party* of whites!

A number of our people immediately went down to see what was doing — myself among them. On our arrival, we found they

of their chiefs to St. Louis, but it is very probable that they were not aware of the large land cession to be undertaken. They apparently thought the important matter at hand was the Cuivre affair about which the Americans had been pressing them.

In ceding land, an Indian nation would normally expect to receive a formal invitation to make a treaty, and the proposed cession would be discussed in advance by the tribal council. The delegation sent to the treaty-making parley would be a large one, consisting of qualified chiefs with their orator, and perhaps many common members of the tribe. But nothing was said about a land cession in the message that Pierre Chouteau sent to the Sauk and Fox, summoning their representatives to St. Louis. In translation it reads as follows:

"My brothers. The great chief of the seventeen great cities of America, having chosen me to maintain peace and union between all the Red skins and the government of the United States, I have in consequence just received the order from the great Chief of our country, who has just arrived from the post of Vincennes, to send for the chiefs of your villages with some important men, and to bring with them those of you who recently killed his children; I enjoin you to come at once, and if some great reasons prevent you from bringing the murderers with you, this is not to prevent you from obeying the orders which I transmit to you. When you carry them out, you will be treated as chiefs and you will go home after having listened to the word of your Father, and then you can make it understood by your elders and your young people; so open your ears and come at once. You will be treated as friends and allies of the United States." (Pierre Chouteau letterbook, Oct. 18, 1804, in MO.)

Chouteau, an Indian agent, sent the message by Louis Honoré, instructing him in a letter of Sept. 18 to "go immediately and get the chiefs and some important men of the Sac and Fox nations. . . ." He also told Honoré to find out how affairs stood between the Indians and the British, "employing only methods of gentleness and persuasion."

Although Black Hawk mentions only four signers, there are five Indian names on the treaty — the fifth being Layowvois. One of the signers, Quashquame or Jumping Fish, repeatedly said in later years that Chouteau had come to the Indian camp at St. Louis and offered to liberate the prisoner in exchange for all

were building a *fort!*[27] The soldiers were busily engaged in cutting timber; and I observed that they took their arms with them, when they went to the woods — and the whole party acted as they would do in an enemy's country! The chiefs held a council with the officers, or head men, of the party — which I did not attend — but understood from them that the war chief had said, that they were building houses for a *trader,* who was coming there to live, and would sell us goods very cheap! and that these soldiers were to remain to keep him company! We were pleased at this information, and hoped it was all true — but we could not believe that all these buildings were intended merely for the accommodation of a trader! Being distrustful of their intentions, we were anxious for them to

the land claimed by the Sauk and Fox east of the Mississippi. Quashquame said he had agreed in part, but did not understand that he was selling any land above the Rock River. (Forsyth's report of Oct. 1, 1832, Draper mss., 9T54–59, in WHI.)

The land described in the treaty and shown on the map above, p. 40, far exceeds the area mentioned by the Secretary of War in authorizing Harrison to act. Harrison was instructed to try for "such sessions on either side of the Illinois, as may entitle them [the Indians] to an annual compensation of five or six hundred dollars; they ought to relinquish all pretensions to any land on the southern side of the Illinois, and a considerable tract on the other side." (*Harrison's Messages and Letters,* I, 101.)

Jefferson explained to the Senate, when he sent the treaty for ratification in December, 1804, that because the Fox had come forward with the Sauk as one tribe, when only the Sauk had been expected, the amount of the annuity was enlarged accordingly. He added, "this cession giving us a perfect title to such a breadth of country on the eastern side of the Mississippi, with a command of the Ouisconsin, strengthens our means of retaining exclusive commerce with the Indians, on the western side of the Mississippi: a right indispensable to the policy of governing those Indians by commerce rather than by arms." (*American State Papers,* Ind. Affairs, I, 693.) The two thousand and some dollars in goods already delivered, mentioned in Art. 2 of the treaty, cannot be identified. Quashquame's statement that he and the others had been drunk may account for most of it. Isaac Galland, who knew Quashquame and his associates, said that this money "was spent by them in the grog-shops of St. Louis, before they left that place. . . . The writer has no doubt, from his own personal knowledge of Quasquaw-ma, that he would have sold to Gov. Harrison, at that time, all the country east of the Rocky Mountains, if it had been required." (Galland's *Chronicles,* Vol. 1, No. 4, p. 53.) Twenty-five years later Quashquame was still trying to live down the treaty. At one council with the Americans in 1829, Keokuk said of him, "This old man is the man who has made us all unhappy."

[27] Fort Madison, on the site of the present town of Fort Madison, Iowa, was erected in 1808 by Lt. Alpha Kingsley.

leave off building, and go down the river again. By this time, a considerable number of Indians had arrived, to see what was doing. I discovered that the whites were alarmed!

Some of our young men watched a party of soldiers, who went out to work, carrying their arms — which were laid aside, before they commenced. Having stole up quietly to the spot, they seized the guns and gave a yell! The party threw down their axes, and ran for their arms, but found them gone! and themselves surrounded! Our young men laughed at them, and returned them their guns.

When this party came to the fort, they reported what had been done, and the war chief made a *serious* affair of it. He called our chiefs to council, inside of his fort. This created considerable excitement in our camp — every one wanted to know what was going to be done — and the picketing which had been put up, being low — every Indian crowded round the fort, and got upon blocks of wood, and old barrels, that they might see what was going on inside. Some were armed with guns, and others with bows and arrows. We used this precaution, seeing that the soldiers had their guns loaded — and having seen them load their *big gun* that morning!

A party of our braves commenced dancing, and proceeded up to the gate, with an intention of going in, but were stopped. The council immediately broke up — the soldiers, with their arms in their hands, rushed out of their rooms, where they had been concealed — the cannon was hauled in front of the gateway — and a soldier came running with fire in his hand, ready to apply the match. Our braves gave way, and all retired to the camp.

There was no preconcerted plan to attack the whites at that time — but I am of opinion now, had our party got into the fort, all the whites would have been killed — as the British soldiers had been at Mackinac [28] many years before.

We broke up our camp, and returned to Rock river. A short

[28] Chippewa and Sauk Indians attacked Fort Michilimackinac during the excitement of a lacrosse game, June 4, 1763, while the garrison was diverted and discipline was relaxed. Most of the defenders of the fort were massacred.

time afterwards, the fort party received a reinforcement — among whom we observed some of our old friends from St. Louis.[29]

Soon after our return from fort Madison, runners came to our village from the *Shawnee Prophet*,[30] (whilst others were despatched by him to the villages of the Winnebagoes,)[31] with invitations for us to meet him on the Wabash. Accordingly a party went from each village.

All of our party returned, among whom came a *Prophet*, who explained to us the bad treatment the different nations of Indians had received from the Americans, by giving them a few presents, and taking their land from them. I remember well his saying, — *"If you do not join your friends on the Wabash, the Americans will take this very village from you!"* I little thought then, that his words would come true! Supposing that he used these arguments merely to encourage us to join him, we agreed that we would not. He then returned to the Wabash, where a party of Winnebagoes had arrived, and preparations were making for war! A battle soon ensued, in which several Winnebagoes were killed.[32] As soon as their nation heard of this battle, and that some of their people had been killed, they started war parties in different directions. One to the mining country; one to Prairie du Chien, and another to fort Madison. This last returned by our village, and exhibited several *scalps* which they had taken. Their success induced several other parties to go against the fort. Myself and several of my band joined the last party, and were determined to take the fort. We arrived in the vicinity during the night. The spies that we had sent out several days before, to watch the movements of those at the garrison, and ascertain their numbers, came to us, and gave the following information: — "That a keel-boat had arrived from below that evening, with seventeen men; that there were about fifty men in

---

[29] Capt. Horatio Stark arrived in late August, 1809, to relieve Kingsley.
[30] The brother of Tecumseh. Also see note, p. 100.
[31] A Siouan tribe, related by language to the Oto, Iowa, and Missouri Indians. Their oldest known range was on the south side of Green Bay, extending inland to Lake Winnebago in present Wisconsin. Population in 1820, about 5,800.
[32] The Battle of Tippecanoe, Nov. 7, 1811.

the fort, and that they marched out every morning at sunrise, to exercise." [33]

It was immediately determined that we should take a position as near as we could, (to conceal ourselves,) to the place where the soldiers would come; and when the signal was given, each man to fire, and then rush into the fort. I dug a hole with my knife, deep enough, (by placing a few weeds around it,) to conceal myself. I was so near to the fort that I could hear the sentinel walking. By day-break, I had finished my work, and was anxiously awaiting the rising of the sun. The drum beat; I examined the priming of my gun, and eagerly watched for the gate to open. It did open — but instead of the troops marching out, a young man came alone. The gate closed after him. He passed close by me — so near that I could have killed him with my knife, but I let him pass. He kept the path towards the river; and had he went one step out of it, he must have come upon us, and would have been killed. He returned immediately, and entered the gate. I would now have rushed for the gate, and entered it with him, but I feared that our party was not prepared to follow me.

The gate opened again — four men came out, and went down to the river after wood. Whilst they were gone, another man came out, and walked towards the river — was fired upon and *killed* by a Winnebago. The others immediately ran for the fort, and two of them were killed. We then took shelter under the bank, out of reach of fire from the fort.

The firing now commenced from both parties, and continued all day. I advised our party to set fire to the fort, and commenced preparing arrows for that purpose. At night we made the attempt, and succeeded to fire the buildings several times, but without effect, as the fire was always instantly extinguished.

[33] Capt. Horatio Stark, in command of the fort, had expressed dissatisfaction with the number of men at his disposal earlier in the year. On Feb. 7, 1812, he wrote to Lt. Col. Daniel Bissell: "I have not men sufficient to post the proper number of Sentries. . . . The aggregate present is forty Six, from which are to be deducted three Privates that can do no Duty four boys and four Waiters.— This makes Duty very hard. . . ." (*Terr. Papers*, 14:521.) Stark was then in his third year as commander of this outpost.

The next day I took my rifle, and shot in two the cord by which they hoisted their flag, and prevented them from raising it again. We continued firing until all our ammunition was expended; and finding that we could not take the fort, returned home, having had one Winnebago killed, and one wounded, during the siege. I have since learned that the trader, who lived in the fort, wounded the Winnebago when he was *scalping* the first man that was killed! The Winnebago recovered, is now living, and is very friendly disposed towards the trader, believing him to be a *great brave!*

Soon after our return home, news reached us that a war was going to take place between the British and the Americans. Runners continued to arrive from different tribes, all confirming the report of the expected war. The British agent, Col. Dixon,[34] was holding *talks* with, and making presents to, the different tribes. I had not made up my mind whether to join the British, or remain neutral. *I had not discovered one good trait in the character of the Americans that had come to the country!* They made *fair promises* but *never fulfilled them!* Whilst the *British* made but few — but we could always *rely upon their word!*

One of our people having killed a Frenchman at Prairie du Chien,[35] the British took him prisoner, and said they would *shoot him* the next day! His family were encamped a short distance below the mouth of the Ouisconsin. He begged for permission to go and see them that night, as he was *to die the next day!* They permitted him to go, after promising to return the next morning by sunrise. He visited his family, which consisted of a wife and six children. I cannot describe their *meeting* and *parting*, to be understood by the whites; as it appears that their feelings are acted upon by certain rules laid down by their *preachers!* — whilst ours are governed only by the monitor within us. He parted from his wife

[34] Robert Dickson, a British trader, was active in recruiting Indians to aid the British in the War of 1812. He was greatly admired by the Indians, and was friendly toward the Americans for a time; in 1807 the Secretary of the Missouri Territory, after issuing him a trading license, said: "I rely greatly on Mr Dickson — by him we shall be correctly informed of whatever passes among the Sieux of River Des Moines & the Iowa . . . he will cooperate most heartily in all our Indian measures." (Bates to Lewis, Nov. 7, 1807, in Marshall, I, 232.)
[35] Prairie du Chien was occupied by the British during 1814-15.

and children, hurried through the prairie to the fort, and arrived in time! The soldiers were ready, and immediately marched out *and shot him down!* I visited his family, and by hunting and fishing, provided for them until they reached their relations.

Why did the Great Spirit ever send the whites to this island, to drive us from our homes, and introduce among us *poisonous liquors, disease and death?* They should have remained on the island where the Great Spirit first placed them. But I will proceed with my story. My memory, however, is not very good, since my late visit to the white people. I have still a buzzing in my ears, from the noise — and may give some parts of my story out of place; but I will endeavor to be correct.

Several of our chiefs and head men were called upon to go to Washington, to see their Great Father. They started; and during their absence, I went to Peoria, on the Illinois river, to see an old friend, a trader,[36] to get his advice. He was a man that always told us the truth, and knew every thing that was going on. When I arrived at Peoria, he was not there, but had gone to Chicago. I visited the Pottawattomie[37] villages, and then returned to Rock

[36] Thomas Forsyth (1771–1833), who since 1804 had been a fur trader at Peoria in partnership with his half-brother, John Kinzie, of Chicago. In 1812 he was made a sub-agent of Indian affairs. Secretly in the pay of the United States during the war, Forsyth feared that word of his spying might get to the pro-British Indians via the French citizens of Peoria. He wrote to Gov. Ninian Edwards, "For God's sake don't mention my name to any person, for if the French get hold of it my life is gone." (*Terr. Papers*, 16:264.) From 1819 to 1830 he was Indian agent at Fort Armstrong.

[37] A tribe of the Algonquian family, related by language to the Chippewa and Ottawa. The traditional homeland of the Potawatomi was the lower peninsula of Michigan, but by about 1765 they had moved into much of northern Illinois and southern Michigan. Between 1836 and 1841 they ceded their lands and moved west of the Mississippi — some to southwestern Iowa and some to Kansas. In 1846 the Iowa band moved to Kansas. Total population between 1765 and 1843 seems to have averaged 2,000 to 2,500.

Both the British and the Americans tried hard to recruit the scattered bands of Potawatomi as allies during the War of 1812. Ninian Edwards instructed Thomas Forsyth at Peoria: "You will insist upon their striking a blow upon some of our enemies as proof of the sincerity of any promises or professions they make." (*Wis. Hist. Coll.*, 11:316–17.) Some of the bands participated, but neither side got much help from the tribe. Robert Dickson wrote in 1814: "The Poutewatamies have always been villians to both parties & will continue so until the end of the Chapter." (*Wis. Hist. Coll.*, 11:290.)

river. Soon after which, our friends returned from their visit to our Great Father — and related what had been said and done. Their Great Father (they said,) wished us, in the event of a war taking place with England, not to interfere on either side — but to remain neutral. He did not want our help — but wished us to hunt and support our families, and live in peace. He said that British traders would not be permitted to come on the Mississippi, to furnish us with goods — but, we would be well supplied by an American trader. Our chiefs then told him that the *British traders* always gave us *credits* in the fall, for guns, powder and goods, to enable us to hunt, and clothe our families. He replied that the trader at fort Madison would have plenty of goods — that we should go there in the fall, and he would supply us *on credit*, as the *British traders had done*. The party gave a good account of what they had seen, and the kind treatment they received.

This information pleased us all very much. We all agreed to follow our Great Father's advice, and not interfere with the war. Our women were much pleased at this good news. Every thing went on cheerfully in our village. We resumed our pastimes of playing ball, horse racing, and dancing, which had been laid aside when this great war was first talked about.

We had fine crops of corn, which were now ripe — and our women were engaged in gathering it, and making *cashes* to contain it. In a short time we were ready to start to fort Madison, to get our supply of goods, that we might proceed to our hunting grounds. We passed merrily down the river — all in high spirits. I had determined to spend the winter at my old favorite hunting ground, on Skunk river, and left part of my corn and meat [38] at its mouth, to take up when I returned: others did the same. Next morning we arrived at the fort, and made our encampment. Myself and principal men paid a visit to the war chief at the fort. He received us kindly, and gave us some tobacco, pipes and provision. The trader came in, and we all rose and shook hands with him — for on him all our dependence was placed, to enable us to hunt, and thereby support our families. We waited a long time, expecting the trader would tell us that he had orders from our Great Father to supply

[38] This word was changed to "mats" in the 1834 edition.

us with goods — but he said nothing on the subject. I got up, and told him, in a short speech, what we had come for — and hoped he had plenty of goods to supply us — and told him that he should be well paid in the spring — and concluded, by informing him, that we had determined to follow our Great Father's advice, and not go to war.

He said that he was happy to hear that we intended to remain at peace. That he had a large quantity of goods; and that, if we made a good hunt, we would be well supplied: but remarked, that *he had received no instructions to furnish us any thing on credit! — nor could he give us any without receiving the pay for them on the spot!*

We informed him what our Great Father had told our chiefs at Washington — and contended that he could supply us if he would — believing that our *Great Father always spoke the truth!* But the war chief said that the trader could not furnish us on credit — and that *he had received no instructions from our Great Father at Washington!* We left the fort dissatisfied, and went to our camp. What was now to be done, we knew not. We questioned the party that brought us the news from our Great Father, that we would get credit for our winter's supplies, at this place. They still told the same story, and insisted upon its truth. Few of us slept that night — all was gloom and discontent!

In the morning, a canoe was seen descending the river — it soon arrived, bearing an express, who brought intelligence that La Gutrie,[39] a *British trader*, had landed at Rock Island, with *two boats* loaded with goods — and requested us to come up immediately — because he had *good news* for us, and a *variety of presents*. The express presented us with tobacco, pipes and wampum.

The news run through our camp like *fire in the prairie*. Our

[39] Edward La Gouthrie, La Guthrie, or Lagoterie, a trader who dealt particularly with the Sauk and was associated with Dickson in encouraging them to fight on the British side. His present of tobacco, pipes, and wampum was modest when compared to the gifts the Indians received on their visits to British territory. One American trader reported seeing an Indian with "an elegant rifle, 25 pounds of powder 50 of lead 3 blankets 3 strouds of cloth, ten shirts and several other articles," given him by the British. (*Harrison's Messages and Letters*, I, 575.)

lodges were soon taken down, and all started for Rock Island. Here ended all hopes of our remaining at peace — having been *forced into* WAR *by being* DECEIVED!

Our party were not long in getting to Rock Island. When we came in sight, and saw tents pitched, we yelled, fired our guns, and commenced beating our drums. Guns were immediately fired at the island, returning our salute, and a *British flag hoisted!* We landed, and were cordially received by La Gutrie — and then smoked the pipe with him! After which he made a speech to us, that had been sent by Colonel Dixon, and gave us a number of handsome presents — a large silk flag, and a keg of rum, and told us to retire — take some refreshments and rest ourselves, as he would have more to say to us on the next day.

We, accordingly, retired to our lodges, (which had been put up in the mean time,) and spent the night. The next morning we called upon him, and told him that we wanted his two boats' load of goods to divide among our people — for which he should be well paid in the spring with furs and peltries. He consented — told us to take them — and do as we pleased with them. Whilst our people were dividing the goods, he took me aside, and informed me that Col. Dixon was at Green Bay with twelve boats, loaded with goods, guns, and ammunition — and wished me to raise a party immediately and go to him. He said that our friend, the trader at Peoria, was callecting the Pottawatomies and would be there before us. I communicated this information to my braves, and a party of two hundred warriors were soon collected and ready to depart.

I paid a visit to the lodge of an old friend, who had been the comrade of my youth, and had been in many war parties with me, but was now crippled, and no longer able to travel. He had a son that I had adopted as my own, who had hunted with me the two preceding winters. I wished my old friend to let him go with me. He objected, saying that he could not get his support if his son left him: that I, (who had always provided for him since he got lame,) would be gone, and he had no other dependence than his son. I offered to leave my son in his place — but he still refused. He said he did not like the war — he had been down the river, and had been well treated by the Americans, and could not fight against them. He had promised to winter near a white settler above Salt river, and must take his son with him. We parted. I soon concluded my arrangements, and started with my party to Green Bay. On our arrival there, we found a large encampment, and were well received by Dixon, and the war chiefs that were with him. He gave us plenty of provisions, tobacco and pipes, and said he would hold a council with us the next day.

In the encampment, I found a large number of Pottowatomies, Kickapoos,[40] Ottawas [41] and Winnebagoes. I visited all their camps, and found them in high spirits. They had all received new guns, ammunition, and a variety of clothing. In the evening a messenger came to me to visit Col. Dixon. I went to his tent, in which were two other war chiefs, and an interpreter. He received me with a hearty shake of the hand, and presented me to the other chiefs, who shook my hand cordially, and seemed much pleased to see me. After I was seated, Col. Dixon said: "Gen. Black Hawk, I sent for you, to explain to you what we are going to do, and the reasons that have brought us here. Our friend, La Gutrie, informs us in the letter you brought from him, what has lately taken place. You will now have to hold us fast by the hand. Your English father has found out that the Americans want to take your country from you — and has sent me and his braves to drive them back to their own country. He has, likewise, sent a large quantity of arms and ammunition — and we want all your warriors to join us." [42]

[40] An Algonquian group, related by language to the Sauk and Fox. In 1667–70 they were in the area that is now Columbia County, Wis., but early in the eighteenth century a portion of the tribe moved down into Illinois territory. They fought on the British side in the War of 1812. Population in 1825, about 2,200.

[41] An Algonquian group most closely related to the Chippewa and Potawatomi. Their earliest known location was Manitoulin Island in Lake Huron, and the northern shore of Georgian Bay, but later they dispersed over a wide area. Pontiac, who led an Indian rebellion against the English colonists, was an Ottawa. Population figures are inadequate because of the scattered condition of the tribe.

[42] It might have been difficult for the Sauk to avoid going to war on the British side. Black Hawk once quoted Dickson as saying, "If you do not immediately strike upon the Americans, I will turn all the other Indians against you and strike you to the ground." (*Michigan Historical Collections*, 16:192–96.) Some

He then placed a medal round my neck, and gave me a paper, (which I lost in the late war,) and a silk flag, saying — "You are to command all the braves that will leave here the day after to-morrow, to join our braves near Detroit."

I told him that I was very much disappointed — as I wanted to descend the Mississippi, and make war upon the settlements. He said he had been "ordered to lay the country waste around St. Louis — that he had been a trader on the Mississippi many years — had always been kindly treated, *and could not consent to send brave men to murder women and children!* That there were no soldiers there to fight; but where he was going to send us, there were a number of soldiers: and, if we defeated them, the Mississippi country should be ours!" I was pleased with this speech; it was spoken by a *brave!*

I inquired about my old friend, the trader, at Peoria, and observed, "that I expected he would have been here before me." He shook his head, and said he "had sent express after express to him, *and had offered him large sums of money,* to come, and bring all the Pottowatomies and Kickapoos with him; but he refused, saying, *'your British father had not money enough to induce him to join us!'* I have now laid a trap for him. I have sent *Gomo,*[43] and a party of Indians, to take him prisoner, and bring him here alive. I expect him in a few days."

The next day, arms and ammunition, tomahawks, knives, and clothing, were given to my band. We had a great feast in the evening; and the morning following, I started with about *five hundred braves,* to join the British army. The British war chief accompanied us. We passed Chicago. The fort had been evacuated by the American soldiers, who had marched for fort Wayne. They were attacked a short distance from that fort, and *defeated!*[44] They had

confirmation of this is found in a statement by Col. Robert McDonall, who said that some of Britain's Indian allies, particularly the Sauk, had been forced into the war. (*Mich. Hist. Coll.*, 16:283–84.)

[43] A Potawatomi chief whose village was on the Illinois River above Peoria. He was loyal to the Americans during the War of 1812, largely due to the efforts of Thomas Forsyth.

[44] The Fort Dearborn massacre, Aug. 15, 1812.

a considerable quantity of powder in the fort at Chicago, which they had *promised to the Indians*; but the night before they marched, they destroyed it. I think it was thrown into the well! If they had fulfilled their word to the Indians, I think they would have gone safe.

On our arrival, I found that the Indians had several prisoners. I advised them to treat them well. We continued our march, and joined the British army below Detroit; and soon after had a fight! [45] The Americans fought well, and drove us with considerable loss! I was surprised at this, as I had been told that the *Americans could not fight!*

Our next movement was against a fortified place. [46] I was stationed, with my braves, to prevent any person going to, or coming from the fort. I found two men taking care of cattle, and took them prisoners. I would not kill them, but delivered them to the British war chief. Soon after, several boats came down the river, full of American soldiers. They landed on the opposite side, took the British batteries, and pursued the soldiers that had left them. They went too far, without knowing the forces of the British, and were *defeated!* I hurried across the river, anxious for an opportunity to show the courage of my braves; but before we reached the ground, all was over! The British had taken many prisoners, *and the Indians were killing them!* I immediately put a stop to it, as I never thought it brave, but cowardly, to kill an unarmed and helpless enemy! [47]

[45] The Battle of Frenchtown on the Raisin River, at the western end of Lake Erie, Jan. 22, 1813, in which the British and the Indians defeated the Kentucky troops of Gen. James Winchester. Indians later said that Winchester would have been the victor if he had held out a while longer. (*Terr. Papers*, 16:326.)

[46] Fort Meigs, on the Maumee River, where on May 1, 1813, Gen. William Henry Harrison was besieged by Gen. Henry Proctor with about 5,000 British troops and Indian allies.

[47] Failure of the British to prevent the torture and slaughter of prisoners by the Indians was one of the factors which moved the House of Representatives to conduct an inquiry "into the spirit and manner in which the war has been waged by the enemy." In a report entitled *Barbarities of the Enemy* . . . the committee wrote, "That these outrages were perpetrated by Indians is neither palliation nor excuse. Every civilized nation is responsible for the conduct of the allies under their command, and while they partake of the advantages of

We remained here some time. I cannot detail what took place, as I was stationed, with my braves, in the woods. It appeared, however, that the British could not take this fort — for we were marched to another some distance off. When we approached it, I found it a small *stockade*, and concluded that there were not many men in it. The British war chief sent a flag — Colonel Dixon carried it, and returned. He said a young war chief commanded, and would not give up *without fighting!* Dixon came to me and said, "you will see, to-morrow, how easily we will take that fort." I was of opinion that they would take it; but when the morning came, I was *disappointed.* The British advanced — commenced an attack, and fought like braves; but by braves in the fort, were *defeated,* and a great number killed![48] The British army were making preparations to retreat. I was now tired of being with them — our success being bad, and having got no plunder. I determined on leaving them and returning to Rock river, to see what had become of my wife and children, as I had not heard from them since I started. That night, I took about twenty of my braves, and left the British camp for home. We met no person on our journey until we reached the Illinois river. Here we found two lodges of Pottowatamies. They received us very friendly, and gave us something to eat; and inquired about their friends that were with the British. They said there had been some fighting on the Illinois, and that my old friend, the trader at Peoria, had been taken prisoner! "By Gomo and his party?" I immediately inquired. They said "no; but by the *Americans,* who came up with two boats. They took him and the French settlers, and then burnt the village of Peoria." [49] They could give

their success, they are equally partaking of the odium of their crimes." (P. 8.) Conscious of such criticism, the British issued orders to their officers that the Indians were to be prevented from committing acts of cruelty and inhumanity. (Cruikshank, 333–34.)

[48] Fort Stephenson, at Lower Sandusky, Ohio, where Maj. George Croghan repulsed the British and Indians on Aug. 2, 1813. Major Croghan was a nephew of George Rogers Clark, and later served under Zachary Taylor in the Mexican War.

[49] The old French village of Peoria was raided by a force of Illinois militia under Capt. Thomas E. Craig, in November, 1812, because Craig believed that some of the French were joining the enemy. The prisoners he took included Antoine LeClaire, father of the interpreter, and Thomas Forsyth. Craig's handling of the Peoria citizens was unauthorized, and later was disapproved

us no news respecting our people on Rock river. In three days more, we were in the vicinity of our village,[50] when I discovered a smoke ascending from a hollow in the bluffs. I directed my party to proceed to the village, as I wished to go alone to the place from whence the smoke proceeded, to see who was there. I approached the spot, and when I came in view of the fire, saw a mat stretched, and an old man sitting under it in sorrow. At any other time, I would have turned away without disturbing him — knowing that he had come there to be *alone*, to humble himself before the Great Spirit, that he might take pity on him! I approached and seated myself beside him. He gave one look at me, and then fixed his eyes on the ground! *It was my old friend!* I anxiously inquired for his son, (my adopted child,) and what had befallen our people? My old comrade seemed scarcely alive — he must have fasted a long time. I lighted my pipe, and put in in his mouth. He eagerly drew a few puffs — cast up his eyes, which met mine, and recognized me. His eyes were glassy! He would again have fallen off into forgetfulness, had I not given him some water, which revived him. I again inquired, "what has befallen our people, and what has become of our son?"

In a feeble voice, he said: "Soon after your departure to join the British, I descended the river with a small party, to winter at the place I told you the white man had requested me to come to. When we arrived, I found a fort built, and the white family that had invited me to come and hunt near them, had removed to it. I then paid a visit to the fort, to tell the white people that myself and little band were friendly, and that we wished to hunt in the vicinity of their fort. The war chief who commanded it, told me, that we might hunt on the Illinois side of the Mississippi, and no

by Gov. Ninian Edwards. (*Terr. Papers*, 17:544.) Forsyth was still bitterly trying to recover his property loss, years after the raid.

[50] Here the 1882 edition contains a passage relating Black Hawk's surprise at finding that a party of Americans had followed him from the British camp. "One of them, more daring than his comrades, had made his way through the thicket on foot, and was just in the act of shooting me when I discovered him. I then ordered him to surrender, marched him into camp, and turned him over to a number of our young men with this injunction: 'Treat him as a brother, as I have concluded to adopt him into our tribe!'" For more of this doubtful incident involving Elijah Kilbourn, see note, p. 124.

person would trouble us. That the horsemen only ranged on the Missouri side, and he had directed them not to cross the river. I was pleased with this assurance of safety, and immediately crossed over and made my winter's camp. Game was plenty; we lived happy, and often talked of you. My boy regretted your absence, and the hardships you would have to undergo. We had been here about two moons, when my boy went out, as usual, to hunt. Night came on, and he did not return! I was alarmed for his safety, and passed a sleepless night. In the morning, my old woman went to the other lodges and gave the alarm — and all turned out in pursuit. There being snow on the ground, they soon came upon his track, and after pursuing it some distance, found he was on the trail of a deer, that led towards the river. They soon came to the place where he had stood and fired, and found a deer hanging upon the branch of a tree, which had been skinned. But here were found the *tracks of white men!* They had taken my boy prisoner. Their tracks led across the river, and then down towards the fort. My friends followed them, and soon found my boy lying dead! He had been most cruelly murdered! His face was shot to pieces — his body stabbed in several places — and his head *scalped!* His arms were tied behind him!"

The old man paused for some time, and then told me that his wife had died on her way up the Mississippi! I took the hand of my old friend in mine, and pledged myself to avenge the death of his son! It was now dark — a terrible storm commenced raging, with heavy torrents of rain, thunder and lightning. I had taken my blanket off and wrapped it around the old man. When the storm abated, I kindled a fire, and took hold of my old friend to remove him near to it — but *he was dead!* I remained with him the balance of the night. Some of my party came early in the morning to look for me, and assisted me in burying him on the peak of the bluff. I then returned to the village with my friends. I visited the grave of my old friend the last time, as I ascended Rock river.

On my arrival at the village, I was met by the chiefs and braves, and conducted to a lodge that had been prepared to receive me.

After eating, I gave an account of what I had seen and done. I explained to them the manner the British and Americans fought. Instead of stealing upon each other, and taking every advantage to *kill the enemy* and *save their own people*, as we do, (which, with us is considered good policy in a war chief,) they march out, in open daylight, and *fight*, regardless of the number of warriors they may lose! After the battle is over, they retire to feast, and drink wine, as if nothing had happened; after which, they make a *statement in writing*, of what they have done — *each party claiming the victory!* and neither giving an account of half the number that have been killed on their own side. They all fought like braves, but would not do to *lead a war party* with us. Our maxim is, "*to kill the enemy*, and *save our own men*." Those chiefs would do to *paddle* a canoe, but not to *steer* it. The Americans shoot better than the British, but their *soldiers* are not so well clothed, or provided for.

The village chief informed me that after I started with my braves and the parties who followed, the nation was reduced to so small a party of fighting men, that they would have been unable to defend themselves, if the Americans had attacked them; that all the women and children, and old men, belonging to the warriors who had joined the British, were left with them to provide for; and that a council was held, which agreed that Quàsh-quà-me, the Lance, and other chiefs, with the old men, women, and children, and such others as chose to accompany them, should descend the Mississippi and go to St. Louis, and place themselves under the protection of the American chief stationed there. They accordingly went down to St. Louis, and were received as the friendly band of our nation — sent up the Missouri, and provided for, whilst their friends were assisting the British.[51]

[51] "The whole amount of Sac's and Foxes, who have gone to the wintering grounds, with a U. States Factor is thought to exceed 1500 souls; besides those contained in 155 canoes which ascended the Missouri on Monday last, near 500 warriors crossed over by land, accompanied by Blondeau their interpreter." (*Missouri Gazette*, Oct. 2, 1813.) These Indians were sent to the Missouri because General Clark feared that in their destitute condition they might be induced to join the British. See Clark's letter to the Secretary of War, *Terr. Papers*, 14:697–98.

Ke-o-kuck[52] was then introduced to me as the war-chief of the braves then in the village. I inquired how he had become a chief. They said that a large armed force was seen by their spies, going towards Peoria; that fears were entertained that they would come upon and attack our village; and that a council had been convened to decide upon the best course to be adopted, which concluded upon leaving the village and going on the west side of the Mississippi, to get out of the way. Ke-o-kuck, during the sitting of the council, had been standing at the door of the lodge, (not being allowed to enter, having never killed an enemy,) where he remained until old Wà-co-me came out. He then told him that he had heard what they had decided upon, and was anxious to be permitted to go in and speak, before the council adjourned! Wà-co-me returned, and asked leave for Ke-o-kuck to come in and make a speech. His request was granted. Ke-o-kuck entered, and addressed the chiefs. He said, "I have heard with sorrow, that you have determined to leave our village, and cross the Mississippi, merely because you have been told that the Americans were seen coming in this direction! Would you leave our village, desert our homes, and fly, before an enemy approaches? Would you leave all — even the graves of our fathers, to the mercy of an enemy, without *trying to defend them?* Give me charge of your warriors; I'll defend the village, and you may sleep in safety!"

[52] Keokuk (He Who Has Been Everywhere), born about 1780 at Rock Island, died in Kansas, 1848. A Sauk who was not born a chief but rose to power through leadership and oratory, he was always considered an adversary by Black Hawk. As leader of the "peace band," he usually yielded to the demands made of him by the United States government.

At a council after the Black Hawk War, Gen. Winfield Scott made him a chief, saying to the Indians, "Look on him in the future as one of your chiefs, obey him and respect him as a chief appointed by the President of the United States; And may the brave Sacs and Foxes ever have among them men as brave in battle, and as wise in council as he who we now raise to the rank of chief." (Minutes of a conference between the U. S. and the Sauk and Fox, Sept. 20, 1832, in the records of the Senate, 22nd Congress, NA in ICC.)

In the *Oquawka Spectator*, June 14, 1848, J. B. Patterson published an obituary in which he said that Keokuk was "in every sense of the word, a great man." In the issue of June 28, criticizing a fellow publisher for calling Keokuk capricious and tyrannical, Patterson said: "Did his long and unchangeable friendship for the whites, and his popularity with his band, indicate *caprice* or a *tyrannical disposition?*"

The council consented that Ke-o-kuck should be a war-chief. He marshalled his braves — sent out spies — and advanced with a party himself, on the trail leading to Peoria. They returned without seeing an enemy. The Americans did not come by our village. All were well satisfied with the appointment of Ke-o-kuck. He used every precaution that our people should not be surprised. This is the manner in which, and the cause of, his receiving the appointment.

I was satisfied, and then started to visit my wife and children. I found them well, and my boys were growing finely. It is not customary for us to say much about our women, as they generally perform their part cheerfully, and *never interfere with business belonging to the men!* This is the only wife I ever had, or ever will have.[53] She is a good woman, and teaches my boys to be *brave!* Here I would have rested myself, and enjoyed the comforts of my lodge, but I could not: I had promised to avenge the death of my adopted son!

I immediately collected a party of thirty braves, and explained to them my object in making this war party — it being to avenge the death of my adopted son, who had been cruelly and wantonly murdered by the whites. I explained to them the pledge I had made his father, and told them that they were the last words that he had heard spoken! All were willing to go with me to fulfil my word. We started in canoes, and descended the Mississippi, until we arrived near the place where fort Madison had stood. It had been abandoned by the whites and burnt; nothing remained but the chimneys.[54] We were pleased to see that the white people had retired from our country. We proceeded down the river again. I

[53] Black Hawk's wife was Asshewequa, or Singing Bird. Thomas Forsyth said that a Sauk might have two, three, or more wives, and that they preferred sisters to insure harmony in the lodge. (Forsyth to Clark, Draper mss., 9T12, in WHI.)
[54] Fort Madison had been evacuated Sept. 3, 1813. Lt. Thomas Hamilton had taken over command from Captain Stark in the summer of 1812, and his position had gradually worsened. In his last communication from the fort, July 18, 1813, he had written, "If . . . the Indians continue to harass me in the manner they appear determined to do, I do not know but I will take the responsibility [for evacuating the fort] on myself. . . . It is impossible for us to do duty long in the manner that I have adopted." (*Annals of Iowa*, 3rd ser., 3 (1897) 97–110.)

landed, with one brave, near Capo Gray;[55] the remainder of the
party went to the mouth of the Quiver. I hurried across to the trail
that led from the mouth of the Quiver to a fort,[56] and soon after
heard firing at the mouth of the creek. Myself and brave concealed
ourselves on the side of the road. We had not remained here long,
before two men riding one horse, came in full speed from the
direction of the sound of the firing. When they came sufficiently
near, we fired; the horse jumped, and both men fell! We rushed
towards them — one rose and ran. I followed him, and was gaining
on him, when he ran over a pile of rails that had lately been made,
seized a stick, and struck at me. I now had an opportunity to see
his face — I knew him! He had been at Quàsh-quà-me's village to
learn his people how to plough. We looked upon him as a good
man. I did not wish to kill him, and pursued him no further. I returned and met my brave; he said he had killed the other man,
and had his *scalp* in his hand! We had not proceeded far, before
we met the man, supposed to be killed, coming up the road, stag-
gering like a drunken man, all covered with blood! This was the
most terrible sight I had ever seen. I told my comrade to *kill him*,
to put him out of his misery! I could not look at him. I passed on,
and heard a rustling in the bushes, and distinctly saw two little
boys concealing themselves! I thought of my own children, and
passed on without noticing them! My comrade here joined me, and
in a little while we met the balance of our party. I told them that
we would be pursued, and directed them to follow me. We crossed
the creek, and formed ourselves in the timber. We had not been
here long, before a party of mounted men rushed at full speed
upon us! I took deliberate aim, and shot the man leading the
party. He fell from his horse lifeless! All my people fired, but without effect. The enemy rushed upon us without giving us time to
reload. They surrounded us, and forced us to run into a deep sink-
hole, at the bottom of which there were some bushes. We loaded
our guns, and awaited the approach of the enemy. They rushed
to the edge of the hole and fired, killing one of our men. We re-

[55] Cap au Gris, a rocky prominence on the east bank of the Mississippi, about
twelve miles above the mouth of the Cuivre (Quiver) River.
[56] Fort Howard, established in 1811 or 1812 by Nathan Boone.

turned the fire instantly, and killed one of their party! We reloaded, and commenced digging holes in the side of the bank to protect ourselves, whilst a party watched the movements of the enemy, expecting that their whole force would be upon us immediately. Some of my warriors commenced singing their *death-songs!* I heard the whites talking — and called to them, 'to come out and fight!' I did not like my situation, and wished the matter settled. I soon heard chopping and knocking. I could not imagine what they were doing. Soon after they run up wheels with a battery on it, and fired down without hurting any of us. I called to them again, and told them if they were '*brave* men, to come down and fight us.' They gave up the siege, and returned to their fort about dusk. There were eighteen in this trap with me. We all got out safe, and found one white man dead on the edge of the sink-hole. They did not remove him, for fear of our fire. We *scalped* him, and placed our dead man upon him! We could not have left him in a better situation, than on an enemy![57]

We had now effected our purpose, and started back by land — thinking it unsafe to return in our canoes. I found my wife and children, and the greater part of our people, at the mouth of the Ioway river. I now determined to remain with my family, and hunt for them; and humble myself before the Great Spirit, and return thanks to him for preserving me through the war!

I made my hunting camp on English river, (a branch of the Ioway.) During the winter a party of Pottowatomies came from the Illinois to pay me a visit — among them was Wàsh-e-own, an old man, that had formerly lived in our village. He informed us, that, in the fall, the Americans had built a fort at Peoria, and had prevented them from going down to the Sangomo to hunt. He said they were very much distressed — that Gomo had returned from the British army, and brought news of their defeat near Malden; and told us that *he* went to the American chief with a flag; gave up fighting, and told the chief that he wished to make

[57] The Battle of the Sink Hole, in which Capt. James Craig was killed at the start and Lt. Edward Spears was killed and scalped at the edge of the sink hole. This incident did not occur immediately after Black Hawk returned from fighting with the British, as he says, but more than a year later — in the spring of 1815.

peace for his nation. The American chief gave him a paper for the war chief at the fort at Peoria, and I visited that fort with Gomo. It was then agreed that there should be no more fighting between the Americans and Pottowatomies; and that two of their chiefs, and eight braves, with five Americans, had gone down to St. Louis to have the peace confirmed. This, said Wàsh-e-own, is good news; for we can now go to our hunting-grounds: and, for my part, I never had any thing to do with this war. The Americans never killed any of our people before the war, nor interfered with our hunting grounds; and I resolved to do nothing against them! I made no reply to these remarks, as the speaker was old, and talked like a child!

We gave the Pottowatomies a feast. I presented Wàsh-e-own with a good horse; my braves gave one to each of his party, and, at parting, they said they wished us to make peace — which we did not promise — but told them that we would not send out war parties against the settlements.

A short time after the Pottowatomies left, a party of thirty braves, belonging to our nation, from the *peace camp* on the Missouri, paid us a visit. They exhibited *five scalps*, which they had taken on the Missouri, and wished us to dance over them, which we willingly joined in. They related the manner in which they had taken these scalps. Myself and braves then showed the two we had taken, near the Quiver, and told them the reason that induced that war party to go out; as well as the manner, and difficulty we had in obtaining these scalps.

They recounted to us all that had taken place — the number that had been killed by the *peace party*, as they were called and recognised — which far surpassed what our warriors, who had joined the British, had done! This party came for the purpose of joining the British! I advised them to return to the peace party, and told them the news that the Pottowatomies had brought. They returned to the Missouri, accompanied by some of my braves, whose families were with the peace party.

After sugar-making was over, in the spring, I visited the Fox village, at the lead mines. They had nothing to do with the war, and were not in mourning. I remained there some days, and spent my time pleasantly with them, in dancing and feasting. I then paid a visit to the Pottowatomie village, on the Illinois river, and learned that Sà-na-tu-wa and Tà-ta-puc-key, had been to St. Louis. Gomo told me "that peace had been made between his people and the Americans, and that seven of his party remained with the war chief to make the peace stronger!" He then told me that "Wàsh-e-own was dead! That he had been to the fort, to carry some wild fowl, to exchange for tobacco, pipes, &c. That he had got some tobacco and a little flour, and left the fort before sundown; but had not proceeded far before he was *shot dead*, by a war chief who had concealed himself near the path, for that purpose! — and than dragged him to the lake and threw him in, where I afterwards found him. I have since given two horses and my rifle to his relations, not to break the peace—which they had agreed to."

I remained some time at the village with Gomo, and went with him to the fort to pay a visit to the war chief. I spoke the Pottowatomie tongue well, and was taken for one of their people by the chief. He treated us very friendly, and said he was very much displeased about the murder of Wàsh-e-own, and would find out, and punish the person that killed him. He made some inquiries about the Sacs, which I answered.

On my return to Rock river, I was informed that a party of soldiers had gone up the Mississippi to build a fort at Prairie du Chien. They had stopped near our village, and appeared to be friendly, and were kindly treated by our people.

We commenced repairing our lodges, putting our village in order, and clearing our cornfields. We divided the fields of the party on the Missouri, among those that wanted, on condition that they should be relinquished to the owners, when they returned from the *peace establishment*. We were again happy in our village: our women went cheerfully to work, and all moved on harmoniously.

Some time afterwards, five or six boats arrived, loaded with soldiers, going to Prairie du Chien, to reinforce the garrison. They appeared friendly, and were well received. We held a council with the war chief. We had no intention of hurting him, or any of his party, or we could easily have defeated them. They remained with us all day, and used, and gave us, plenty of whisky! During the night a party arrived, (who came down Rock river,) and brought us six kegs of powder! They told us that the British had gone to Prairie du Chien, and taken the fort, and wished us to join them again in the war, which we agreed to. I collected my warriors, and determined to pursue the boats, which had sailed with a fair wind. If we had known the day before, we could easily have taken them all, as the war chief used no precautions to prevent it. I immediately started with my party, by land, in pursuit — thinking that some of their boats might get aground, or that the Great Spirit would put them in our power, if he wished them taken, and their people killed! About half way up the rapids, I had a full view of the boats, all sailing with a strong wind. I soon discovered that one boat was badly managed, and was suffered to be driven ashore by the wind. They landed, by running hard aground, and lowered their sail. The others passed on. This boat the Great Spirit gave us! We approached it cautiously, and fired upon the men on shore. All that could, hurried aboard, but they were unable to push off, being fast aground. We advanced to the river's bank, under cover, and commenced firing at the boat. Our balls passed through the plank and did execution, as I could hear them screaming in the boat! I encouraged my braves to continue firing. Several guns were fired from the boat, without effect. I prepared my bow and arrows to *throw fire to the sail*, which was lying on the boat; and, after two or three attempts, succeeded in setting the sail on fire.

The boat was soon in flames! About this time, one of the boats that had passed, returned, dropped anchor, and swung in close to the boat on fire, and took off all the people, except those killed and badly wounded. We could distinctly see them passing from one boat to the other, and fired on them with good aim. *We wounded the war chief in this way!* Another boat now came down, dropped her anchor, which did not take hold, and was drifted ashore! The other boat cut her cable and rowed down the river, leaving their comrades without attempting to assist them. We then commenced an attack upon this boat, and fired several rounds.

They did not return the fire. We thought they were afraid, or had but a small number on board. I therefore ordered a rush to the boat. When we got near, they *fired*, and killed two of our people, being all that we lost in the engagement. Some of their men jumped out and pushed off the boat, and thus got away without losing a man! I had a good opinion of this war chief — he managed so much better than the others. It would give me pleasure to shake him by the hand.[58]

We now put out the fire on the captured boat, to save the cargo; when a skiff was discovered coming down the river. Some of our people cried out, "here comes an express from Prairie du Chien!" We hoisted the *British flag*, but they would not land. They turned their little boat around, and rowed up the river. We directed a few shots at them, in order to bring them *to;* but they were so far off that we could not hurt them. I found several barrels of whisky on the captured boat, and knocked in their heads and emptied out the *bad medicine!* I next found a box full of small bottles and packages, which appeared to be *bad medicine* also; such as the *medicine-men* kill the white people with when they get sick. This I threw into the river; and continuing my search for plunder, found several guns, large barrels full of clothing, and some cloth lodges, all of which I distributed among my warriors. We now disposed of the dead, and returned to the Fox village, opposite the lower end of Rock Island; where we put up our new lodges and hoisted the British flag. A great many of our braves were dressed in the uniform clothing which we had taken, which gave our encampment the appearance of a regular camp of soldiers! We placed our sentinels, and commenced dancing over the scalps

[58] The man was Lt. John Campbell, in command of the little group that was heading for Prairie du Chien. The report of his defeat at the hands of the Indians, July 21, 1814, was hailed by the newly established British force at Prairie du Chien. When the commander, Col. William McKay, received the news he wrote a jubilant account to the commander at Michilimackinac, July 27, praising the Indians. ". . . the Sauks, Renards and Kikapoos were engaged in this Action, they lost 2 Men & one Woman kill'd — to give an idea how disperate the indians were, the women even jumped on board with their Hoes &ᶜᵃ, some breaking heads, other breaking casks, some trying to cut Holes in her bottom to sink her. . . ." (Champlain Society, 15:264.)

we had taken. Soon after, several boats passed down; among them, a large boat carrying *big guns!* Our young men followed them some distance, firing at them, but could not do much damage, more than to frighten them. We were now certain that the fort at Prairie du Chien had been taken, as this large boat went up with the first party, who built the fort.

In the course of the day some of the British came down in a small boat; they had followed the large one, thinking she would get fast in the rapids, in which case they were certain of taking her. They had summoned her on the way down to surrender, but she refused; and now, that she had passed over the rapids in safety, all hope of taking her had vanished.

The British landed a *big gun*, and gave us three soldiers to manage it. They complimented us for our bravery in taking the boat, and told us what they had done at Prairie du Chien; gave us a keg of rum, and joined with us in our dancing and feasting! We gave them some things which we had taken from the boat — particularly books and papers. They started the next morning, after promising to return in a few days with a large body of soldiers.

We went to work, under the directions of the men left with us, and dug up the ground in two places, to put the *big gun* in, that the men might remain in with it, and be safe. We then sent *spies* down the river to reconnoitre, who sent word by a runner, that several boats were coming up, filled with men. I marshalled my forces, and was soon ready for their arrival, and resolved to fight — as we had not yet had a fair fight with the Americans during the war. The boats arrived in the evening, and stopped at a small willow island, nearly opposite to us. During the night we removed our *big gun* further down, and at daylight next morning, commenced firing. We were pleased to see that almost every fire took effect, striking the boats nearly every shot. They pushed off as quick as possible; and I expected would land and give a fight. I was prepared to meet them — but was soon *sadly disappointed!* — the boats having all started down the river. A party of braves followed to watch where they landed; but they did not stop until they got below the Des Moines rapids, when they landed, and commenced building a fort.[59]

I collected a few braves, and started to the place where it was reported they were making a fort. I did not want a fort in our country, as we wished to go down in the fall, to the Two-River country, to hunt—it being our best hunting ground; and we concluded, that if this fort was established, we should be prevented from going to our hunting ground. I arrived in the vicinity of the fort in the evening, and stopped for the night, on the peak of a high bluff. We made no fire, for fear of being observed. Our young men kept watch by turns, whilst the others slept. I was very tired, and soon went to sleep. The Great Spirit, during my slumber, told me to go down the bluff to a creek — that I would there find a hollow tree cut down; to look into the top of it, and I would see a large *snake*— to observe the direction he was looking, and I would see the enemy close by, and unarmed. In the morning, I communicated to my braves what the Great Spirit had told me; and took one of them and went down a hollow that led to the creek, and soon came in sight of the place, on an opposite hill, where they were building the fort. I saw a great many men. We crawled cautiously on our hands and knees, until we got into the bottom — then, through the grass and weeds, until we reached the bank of the creek. Here I found a tree that had been cut down. I looked in the top of it, and saw a large snake, with his head raised, looking across the creek. I raised myself cautiously, and discovered, nearly opposite to me, two war chiefs, walking arm-in-arm, without guns. They turned, and walked back towards the place where the men were working at the fort. In a little while they returned, walking immediately towards the spot where we lay concealed — but did not come as near as before. If they had, they would have been killed — for each of us had a good rifle. We crossed the creek, and crawled to a bunch

[59] Black Hawk did not know at the time that he was battling with a future Great Father. The eight boats contained a detachment of troops commanded by Zachary Taylor. Aided by the British gunners and their weapon, the Indians routed the boats. The fort which Taylor built in the fall of 1814, after his encounter with Black Hawk, was Fort Johnson, near what is now Warsaw, Illinois. It was abandoned within a few weeks.

of bushes. I again raised myself a little, to see if they were coming; but they went into the fort. By this they saved their lives.

We recrossed the creek, and I returned alone — going up the hollow we came down. My brave went down the creek; and, on rising a hill to the left of the one we came down, I could plainly see the men at work; and discovered, in the bottom, near the mouth of the creek, a sentinel walking. I watched him attentively, to see if he perceived my companion, who had gone towards him. The sentinel walked first one way and then back again. I observed my brave creeping towards him. The sentinel stopped for some time, and looked in the direction where my brave was concealed. He laid still, and did not move the grass; and, as the sentinel turned to walk, my brave fired and he fell! I looked towards the fort, and saw that they were all in confusion — running in every direction — some down a steep bank to a boat. My comrade joined me, and we returned to the rest of our party, and all hurried back to Rock river, where we arrived in safety at our village. I hung up my *medicine bag*, put away my rifle and spear, and felt as if I should not want them again, as I had no wish to raise any more war parties against the whites, without they gave new provocation. Nothing particular happened from this time until spring, except news that the fort below the rapids had been abandoned and burnt by the Americans.

Soon after I returned from my wintering ground, we received information that *peace* had been made between the British and Americans, and that *we* were required to make peace also — and were invited to go down to Portage des Sioux,[60] for that purpose. Some advised that we should go down — others that we should not. No-mite, our principal civil chief, said he would go, as soon as the Foxes came down from the Mines. They came, and we all started from Rock river. We had not gone far, before our chief was taken sick. We stopped with him at the village on Henderson river. The Foxes went on, and we were to follow as soon as our

[60] A village founded in 1799 on the west bank of the Mississippi, about six miles above the mouth of the Missouri. The Sioux are said once to have escaped an ambush by making a portage there. That is, they carried their canoes and supplies overland between the two rivers.

chief got better; but he continued to get worse, and died. His brother now became the principal chief. He refused to go down — saying, that if he started, he would be taken sick and die, as his brother had done — which was reasonable! We all concluded, that none of us would go at this time.[61]

The Foxes returned. They said they "had smoked the *pipe of peace* with the Americans, and expected that a war party would be sent against us, because we did not go down. This I did not believe; as the Americans had always *lost* by their war parties that came against us.

La Gutrie, and other British traders, arrived at our village on Rock river, in the fall. La Gutrie told us, that we must go down and make peace — that it was the wish of our English father. He said he wished us to go down to the Two-River country[62] to winter — where game was plenty, as there had been no hunting there for several years.

[61] Thus Black Hawk and his band failed to sign the treaties of Sept. 13 and 14, 1815, at Portage des Sioux, which were signed by the Missouri Sauk and by the Fox. The reason he gives for not signing conflicts with the tenor of documents in *American State Papers*, Ind. Affairs, II, 7–10, in which the commissioners complain to the Secretary of War about the hostility and non-cooperative attitude of the Rock River Sauk, and their resistance to signing a treaty.

Instead of signing, the Sauk went to confer with the British in Canada. They complained to the British that they had been insulted by the Americans, and Black Hawk said, "I hope I may not be obliged to dig up my Hatchet. I know these Big Knives have sweet tongues and fear they have cheated us all." (*Mich. Hist. Coll.*, 16:192–96.)

As with previous treaties, there was some confusion among the Indians. Forsyth wrote, "In a Conversation I had with the Interpreter from Fort Clark who was here a few days ago, he informs me that the Indians told him that the treaty was Smoothly done, without any mention of lands, and immediately afterwards people sent to measure their lands which Surprises them much —" (*Terr. Papers*, 17:260.)

Two weeks before the treaty the Potawatomi had sent a message to President Madison, objecting to the fact that the Sauk had sold lands in the treaty of 1804 which were Potawatomi property, and to the reports that white settlers were now going to occupy some of the area. The message said that "no Part of this River [the Illinois] does or ever did belong to the Sacks. . . ." (*Terr. Papers*, 17:228.) It became necessary to negotiate separately with the Potawatomi for these lands, since they were a part of the Illinois Military Tract which had been opened to veterans of the War of 1812 as a land bounty reward for military service.

[62] An area north and west of the present city of Hannibal, Mo.

Having heard that a principal war chief, with troops, had come up, and commenced building a fort [63] near Rapids des Moines, we consented to go down with the traders, to see the American chief, and tell him the reason why we had not been down sooner. We arrived at the head of the rapids. Here the traders left their goods and boats, except one, in which they accompanied us to the Americans. We visited the war chief, (he was on board of a boat,) and told him what we had to say — explaining the reason we had not been down sooner. He appeared angry, and talked to La Gutrie for some time. I inquired of him, what the war chief said? He told me that he was threatening to hang him up on the yard-arm of his boat. "But," said he, "I am not afraid of what he says. He dare not put his threats into execution. I have done no more than I had a right to do, as a British subject."

I then addressed the chief, asking permission for ourselves and some Menomonees,[64] to go down to the Two-River country to hunt. He said, *we* might go down, but must return before the ice made, as he did not intend that we should winter below the fort. "But," said he, "what do you want the Menomonees to go with you for?" I did not know, at first, what reply to make — but told him that they had a great many *pretty squaws* with them, and we wished them to go with us on that account! He consented. We all started down the river, and remained *all winter*, as we had no intention of returning before spring, when we asked leave to go. We made a good hunt. Having loaded our traders' boats with furs and peltries, they started to Mackinac, and we returned to our village.

There is one circumstance which I omitted to mention in its proper place. It does not relate to myself or people, but to my friend Gomo, the Pottowatomie chief. He came to Rock river to

[63] Fort Edwards, on the east side of the Mississippi opposite the mouth of the Des Moines River, near where Zachary Taylor had erected the temporary Fort Johnson in 1814.

[64] The Menominee are an Algonquian tribe, related by language to the Cree and Fox, and originally found near the Menominee River in Wisconsin. The French called them Folles Avoines, or wild rice people, because they subsisted mainly on the wild rice of the lakes. Population estimates in the eighteenth century: from 1,600 to 1,900.

pay me a visit. During his stay, he related to me the following story:

"The war chief at Peoria is a very good man; he always speaks the truth, and treats our people well. He sent for me one day, and told me that he was nearly out of provision, and wished me to send my young men out to hunt, to supply his fort. I promised to do so; and immediately returned to my camp, and told my young men the wishes and wants of the war chief. They readily agreed to go and hunt for our friend; and soon returned with about twenty deer. They carried them to the fort, laid them down at the gate, and returned to our camp. A few days afterwards, I went again to the fort to see if they wanted more meat. The chief gave me some powder and lead, and said he wished me to send my hunters out again. When I returned to my camp, and told my young men that the chief wanted more meat, Má-ta-táh, one of my principal braves, said he would take a party and go across the Illinois, about one day's travel, where game was plenty, and make a good hunt for our friend, the war chief. He took eight hunters with him; his wife and several other squaws accompanied them. They had travelled about half the day in the prairie, when they discovered a party of white men coming towards them with a drove of cattle. Our hunters apprehended no danger, or they would have kept out of the way of the whites, (who had not yet perceived them.) Má-ta-táh changed his course, as he wished to meet and speak to the whites. As soon as the whites saw our party, some of them put off at full speed, and came up to our hunters. Má-ta-táh gave up his gun to them, and endeavored to explain to them that he was friendly, and was hunting for the war chief. They were not satisfied with this, but fired at and wounded him. He got into the branch of a tree that had been blown down, to keep the horses from running over him. He was again fired on by several guns and badly wounded. He found that he would be murdered, (if not mortally wounded already,) and sprung at the nearest man to him, seized his gun, and shot him from his horse. He then fell, covered with blood from his wounds, and almost instantly expired!

"The other hunters, being in the rear of Má-ta-táh, seeing that the whites had killed him, endeavored to make their escape. They

were pursued, and nearly all the party *murdered!* My youngest
brother brought me the news in the night, he having been with
the hunters, and got but slightly wounded. He said the whites had
abandoned their cattle, and gone back towards the settlement. The
remainder of the night was spent in lamenting for the death of
our friends. At day-light, I blacked my face, and started to the fort
to see the war chief. I met him at the gate, and told him what had
happened. His countenance changed; I could see sorrow depicted
in it for the death of my people. He tried to persuade me that I was
mistaken, as he 'could not believe that the whites would act so
cruelly.' But when I convinced him, he told me that those '*cowards*
who had murdered my people should be punished.' I told him that
my people would have *revenge* — that they would not trouble any
of his people of the fort, as we did not blame him or any of his
soldiers — but that a party of my braves would go towards the
Wabash to avenge the death of their friends and relations. The
next day I took a party of hunters and killed several deer, and left
them at the fort gate as I passed."

Here Gomo ended his story. I could relate many similar ones
that have come within my own knowledge and observation; but I
dislike to look back and bring on sorrow afresh. I will resume
my narrative.

The great chief[65] at St. Louis having sent word for us to go
down and confirm the treaty of peace, we did not hesitate, but
started immediately, that we might smoke the *peace-pipe* with him.
On our arrival, we met the great chiefs in council. They explained
to us the words of our Great Father at Washington, accusing us
of heinous crimes and divers misdemeanors, particularly in not
coming down when first invited. We knew very well that *our Great
Father had deceived us*, and thereby *forced* us to join the British,
and could not believe that he had put this speech into the mouths
of these chiefs to deliver to us. I was not a civil chief, and consequently made no reply: but our chiefs told the commissioners that
"what they had said was a *lie!* — that our Great Father had sent
no such speech, he knowing the situation in which we had been
placed had been *caused by him!*" The white chiefs appeared very

[65] William Clark.

angry at this reply, and said they "would break off the treaty with us, and *go to war*, as they would not be insulted."

Our chiefs had no intention of insulting them, and told them so — "that they merely wished to explain to them that *they had told a lie*, without making them angry; in the same manner that the whites do, when they do not believe what is told them!" The council then proceeded, and the pipe of peace was smoked.

Here, for the first time, I touched the goose quill to the treaty— not knowing, however, that, by that act, I consented to give away my village. Had that been explained to me, I should have opposed it, and never would have signed their treaty, as my recent conduct will clearly prove.[66]

What do we know of the manner of the laws and customs of the white people? They might buy our bodies for dissection, and we would touch the goose quill to confirm it, without knowing what we are doing. This was the case with myself and people in touching the goose quill the first time.

We can only judge of what is proper and right by our standard of right and wrong, which differs widely from the whites, if I have been correctly informed. The whites *may do bad* all their lives, and then, if they are *sorry for it* when about to die, *all is well!* But with us it is different: we must continue throughout our lives to do what we conceive to be good. If we have corn and meat, and know of a family that have none, we divide with them. If we have more blankets than sufficient, and others have not enough, we must give to them that want. But I will presently explain our customs, and the manner we live.

We were friendly treated by the white chiefs, and started back to our village on Rock river. Here we found that troops had arrived to build a fort at Rock Island.[67] This, in our opinion, was

[66] This was the treaty of May 13, 1816, in which the Sauk of the Rock River unconditionally assented to and confirmed the treaty of 1804 — as the Missouri Sauk and the Fox had done the year before. And once more there was misunderstanding, as shown by Black Hawk's account.

[67] Construction of Fort Armstrong on Rock Island was begun May 10, 1816. Maj. Morrell Marston described it as follows in a report to Maj. Gen. Alexander Macomb, in 1819: "This fort is about 270 feet square, with three block houses mounting three 6-pounders. The barracks are well constructed of hewn timber, and are sufficiently extensive to quarter three companies. The magazine is of

a contradiction to what we had done — "to prepare for war in time
of peace." We did not, however, object to their building the fort
on the island, but we were very sorry, as this was the best island
on the Mississippi, and had long been the resort of our young
people during the summer. It was our garden (like the white people have near to their big villages) which supplied us with
strawberries, blackberries, gooseberries, plums, apples, and nuts
of different kinds; and its waters supplied us with fine fish, being
situated in the rapids of the river. In my early life, I spent many
happy days on this island. A good spirit had care of it, who lived
in a cave in the rocks immediately under the place where the fort
now stands, and has often been seen by our people. He was white,
with large wings like a *swan's*, but ten times larger. We were particular not to make much noise in that part of the island which
he inhabited, for fear of disturbing him. But the noise of the fort
has since driven him away, and no doubt a *bad spirit* has taken his
place!

Our village was situate on the north side of Rock river, at the
foot of its rapids, and on the point of land between Rock river
and the Mississippi. In its front, a prairie extended to the bank
of the Mississippi; and in our rear, a continued bluff, gently ascending from the prairie.[68] On the side of this bluff we had our
corn-fields, extending about two miles up, running parallel with
the Mississippi; where we joined those of the Foxes whose village
was on the bank of the Mississippi, opposite the lower end of Rock
island, and three miles distant from ours. We had about eight
hundred acres in cultivation, including what we had on the islands
of Rock river. The land around our village, uncultivated, was

stone and well built. The commanding officer's quarters consist of a center
two-story building 28 feet in length, with wings of one story 15 feet in length,
and piazzas built in front and rear." (In Tucker, Plate XLIV.)

Caleb Atwater, dealing with the Indians for mineral rights, was apprehensive
about the location of the fort in the event of war with the British. "The fort
on Rock Island, is commanded by hills on both sides of it, and could not stand
an hour against an enemy with cannon posted on the heights." (Atwater, 176.)
[68] In the 1882 edition the following sentence appears here: "On its highest peak
our Watch Tower was situated, from which we had a fine view for many miles
up and down Rock River, and in every direction." Also see note on p. 95 below.

covered with blue-grass, which made excellent pasture for our horses. Several fine springs broke out of the bluff, near by, from which we were supplied with good water. The rapids of Rock river furnished us with an abundance of excellent fish, and the land, being good, never failed to produce good crops of corn, beans, pumpkins, and squashes. We always had plenty — our children never cried with hunger, nor our people were never in want. Here our village had stood for more than a hundred years, during all which time we were the undisputed possessors of the valley of the Mississippi, from the Ouisconsin to the Portage des Sioux, near the mouth of the Missouri, being about seven hundred miles in length.

At this time we had very little intercourse with the whites, except our traders. Our village was healthy, and there was no place in the country possessing such advantages, nor no hunting grounds better than those we had in possession. If another prophet had come to our village in those days, and told us what has since taken place, none of our people would have believed him. What! to be driven from our village and hunting grounds, and not even permitted to visit the graves of our forefathers, our relations, and friends?

This hardship is not known to the whites. With us it is a custom to visit the graves of our friends, and keep them in repair for many years. The mother will go alone to weep over the grave of her child! The brave, with pleasure, visits the grave of his father, after he has been successful in war, and re-paints the post that shows where he lies! There is no place like that where the bones of our forefathers lie, to go to when in grief. Here the Great Spirit will take pity on us!

But, how different is our situation now, from what it was in those days! Then we were as happy as the buffalo on the plains — but now, we are as miserable as the hungry, howling wolf in the prairie! But I am digressing from my story. Bitter reflection crowds upon my mind, and must find utterance.

When we returned to our village in the spring, from our wintering grounds, we would finish trading with our traders, who always followed us to our village. We purposely kept some of our fine furs for this trade; and, as there was great opposition among them,

who should get these skins, we always got our goods cheap.[69] After
this trade was over, the traders would give us a few kegs of rum,
which was generally promised in the fall, to encourage us to make
a good hunt, and not go to war. They would then start with their
furs and peltries for their homes. Our old men would take a frolic,
(at this time our young men never drank.) When this was ended,
the next thing to be done was to bury our dead, (such as had died
during the year.) This is a great *medicine feast*. The relations of
those who have died, give all the goods they have purchased, as
presents to their friends — thereby reducing themselves to poverty,
to show the Great Spirit that they are humble, so that he will take
pity on them. We would next open the cashes, and take out corn
and other provisions, which had been put up in the fall, — and then
commence repairing our lodges. As soon as this is accomplished,
we repair the fences around our fields, and clean them off, ready
for planting corn. This work is done by our women. The men,
during this time, are feasting on dried venison, bear's meat, wild
fowl, and corn, prepared in different ways; and recounting to each
other what took place during the winter.

Our women plant the corn, and as soon as they get done, we
make a feast, and dance the *crane* dance, in which they join us,
dressed in their best, and decorated with feathers. At this feast
our young braves select the young woman they wish to have for a
wife. He then informs his mother, who calls on the mother of the
girl, when the arrangement is made, and the time appointed for
him to come. He goes to the lodge when all are asleep, (or pretend

[69] Maj. Morrell Marston told the Rev. Jedediah Morse that in the winter of
1819–20 the five traders of the Sauk and Fox collected these amounts of furs:
2,760 beaver skins; 922 otter; 13,440 raccoon; 12,900 muskrat; 500 mink; 200
wildcat; 680 bear; 28,680 deer. They also collected 286,800 pounds of deer
tallow, 3,000 pounds of feathers, and 1,000 pounds of beeswax. (Morse, 126.)

"The articles of merchandise which the traders take with them to the Indian
country, are as follows: blankets . . . ; common blue stroud; common red
stroud; blue cloth, scarlet cloth, calicoes, domestic cottons, rifle and shot gun,
gunpowder, flints and lead; knives of different kinds; looking glasses, vermilion,
verdigris; copper, brass, and tin kettles; beaver and muskrat traps; fine and
common bridles and spurs; silver works, needles and thread, wampum, horses,
tomahawks, and half axes, &c." (Forsyth to the Secretary of War, Oct. 24, 1831,
in Missouri Historical Society's *Glimpses of the Past*, 9 (1942) 75.)

to be,) lights his matches, which have been provided for the purpose, and soon finds where his intended sleeps. He then awakens her, and holds the light to his face that she may know him — after which he places the light close to her. If she blows it out, the ceremony is ended, and he appears in the lodge the next morning, as one of the family. If she does not blow out the light, but leaves it to burn out, he retires from the lodge. The next day he places himself in full view of it, and plays his flute. The young women go out, one by one, to see who he is playing for. The tune changes, to let them know that he is not playing for them. When his intended makes her appearance at the door, he continues his *courting* tune, until she returns to the lodge. He then gives over playing, and makes another trial at night, which generally turns out favorable. During the first year they ascertain whether they can agree with each other, and can be happy — if not, they part, and each looks out again. If we were to live together and disagree, we should be as foolish as the whites. No indiscretion can banish a woman from her parental lodge — no difference how many children she may bring home, she is always welcome — the kettle is over the fire to feed them.

The crane dance often lasts two or three days. When this is over, we feast again, and have our *national* dance. The large square in the village is swept and prepared for the purpose. The chiefs and old warriors, take seats on mats which have been spread at the upper end of the square — the drummers and singers come next, and the braves and women form the sides, leaving a large space in the middle. The drums beat, and the singers commence. A warrior enters the square, keeping time with the music. He shows the manner he started on a war party — how he approached the enemy — he strikes, and describes the way he killed him. All join in applause. He then leaves the square, and another enters and takes his place. Such of our young men as have not been out in war parties, and killed an enemy, stand back ashamed — not being able to enter the square. I remember that I was ashamed to look where our young women stood, before I could take my stand in the square as a warrior.

What pleasure it is to an old warrior, to see his son come forward and relate his exploits — it makes him feel young, and induces him to enter the square, and "fight his battles o'er again."

This national dance makes our warriors. When I was travelling last summer, on a steam boat, on a large river, going from New York to Albany, I was shown the place where the Americans dance their national dance [West Point]; where the old warriors recount to their young men, what they have done, to stimulate them to go and do likewise. This surprised me, as I did not think the whites understood our way of making braves.

When our national dance is over — our corn-fields hoed, and every weed dug up, and our corn about knee-high, all our young men would start in a direction towards sun-down, to hunt deer and buffalo — being prepared, also, to kill Sioux,[70] if any are found on our hunting grounds — a part of our old men and women to the lead mines to make lead — and the remainder of our people start to fish, and get mat stuff. Every one leaves the village, and remains about forty days. They then return: the hunting party bringing in dried buffalo and deer meat, and sometimes *Sioux scalps*, when they are found trespassing on our hunting grounds. At other times they are met by a party of Sioux too strong for them, and are driven in. If the Sioux have killed the Sacs last, they expect to be retaliated upon, and will fly before them, and vice versa. Each party knows that the other has a right to retaliate, which induces those who have killed last, to give way before their enemy — as neither wish to strike, except to avenge the death of their relatives. All our wars are predicated by the relatives of those killed; or by aggressions upon our hunting grounds.

The party from the lead mines bring lead, and the others dried fish, and mats for our winter lodges. Presents are now made by each party; the first, giving to the others dried buffalo and deer,

[70] The Sioux or Dakota are a related group of tribes, of Siouan language stock. When first noted by the French in 1640 they were living in the vicinity of Sault Ste Marie, but are associated in American history with the northern Great Plains and the western prairies. In 1780 their estimated population was 25,000 and there are now about 46,000 living on reservations in Minnesota, Nebraska, Montana, and the Dakotas.

and they, in exchange, presenting them with lead, dried fish and mats.

This is a happy season of the year — having plenty of provisions, such as beans, squashes, and other produce, with our dried meat and fish, we continue to make feasts and visit each other, until our corn is ripe. Some lodge in the village makes a feast daily, to the Great Spirit. I cannot explain this so that the white people would comprehend me, as we have no regular standard among us. Every one makes his feast as he thinks best, to please the Great Spirit, who has the care of all beings created. Others believe in two Spirits: one good and one bad, and make feasts for the Bad Spirit, *to keep him quiet!* If they can make peace with him, the Good Spirit will not hurt them! For my part, I am of opinion, that so far as we have *reason*, we have a right to use it, in determining what is right or wrong; and should pursue that path which we believe to be right — believing, that "whatever is, is right." If the Great and Good Spirit wished us to believe and do as the whites, he could easily change our opinions, so that we would see, and think, and act as they do. We are *nothing* compared to His power, and we feel and know it. We have men among us, like the whites, who pretend to know the right path, but will not consent to show it without *pay!* I have no faith in their paths — but believe that every man must make his own path!

When our corn is getting ripe, our young people watch with anxiety for the signal to pull roasting-ears — as none dare touch them until the proper time. When the corn is fit to use, another great ceremony takes place, with feasting, and returning thanks to the Great Spirit for giving us corn.

I will here relate the manner in which corn first came. According to tradition, handed down to our people, a beautiful woman was seen to descend from the clouds, and alight upon the earth, by two of our ancestors, who had killed a deer, and were sitting by a fire, roasting a part of it to eat. They were astonished at seeing her, and concluded that she must be hungry, and had smelt the meat — and immediately went to her, taking with them a piece of the roasted venison. They presented it to her, and she eat — and told them to return to the spot where she was sitting, at the end of one year, and they would find a reward for their kindness and generosity. She then ascended to the clouds, and disappeared. The two men returned to their village, and explained to the nation what they had seen, done, and heard — but were laughed at by their people. When the period arrived, for them to visit this consecrated ground, where they were to find a reward for their attention to the beautiful woman of the clouds, they went with a large party, and found, where her right hand had rested on the ground, *corn* growing — and where the left hand had rested, *beans* — and immediately where she had been seated, *tobacco*.

The two first have, ever since, been cultivated by our people, as our principal provisions — and the last used for smoking. The white people have since found out the latter, and seem to relish it as much as we do — as they use it in different ways, viz. smoking, snuffing and eating!

We thank the Great Spirit for all the benefits he has conferred upon us. For myself, I never take a drink of water from a spring, without being mindful of his goodness.

We next have our great ball play — from three to five hundred on a side, play this game. We play for horses, guns, blankets, or any other kind of property we have. The successful party take the stakes, and all retire to our lodges in peace and friendship.

We next commence horse-racing, and continue our sport and feasting, until the corn is all secured. We then prepare to leave our village for our hunting grounds. The traders arrive, and give us credit for such articles as we want to clothe our families, and enable us to hunt. We first, however, hold a council with them, to ascertain the price they will give us for our skins, and what they will charge us for goods. We inform them where we intend hunting — and tell them where to build their houses. At this place, we deposit part of our corn, and leave our old people. The traders have always been kind to them, and relieved them when in want. They were always much respected by our people — and never since we have been a nation, has one of them been killed by any of our people.

We disperse, in small parties, to make our hunt, and as soon as it is over, we return to our traders' establishment, with our skins, and remain feasting, playing cards and other pastimes, until near the close of the winter. Our young men then start on the beaver hunt; others to hunt raccoons and muskrats — and the remainder of our people go to the sugar camps to make sugar. All leave our encampment, and appoint a place to meet on the Mississippi, so that we may return to our village together, in the spring. We always spent our time pleasantly at the sugar camp. It being the season for wild fowl, we lived well, and always had plenty, when the hunters came in, that we might make a feast for them. After this is over, we return to our village, accompanied, sometimes, by our traders. In this way, the year rolled round happily. But these are times that were! [71]

On returning, in the spring, from our hunting ground, I had the pleasure of meeting our old friend, the trader of Peoria, at Rock Island. He came up in a boat from St. Louis, not as a trader, as in times past, but as our *agent*. We were all pleased to see him. He told us, that he narrowly escaped falling into the hands of Dixon. He remained with us a short time, gave us good advice, and then returned to St. Louis.

The Sioux having committed depredations on our people, we sent out war parties that summer, who succeeded in killing *fourteen*. I paid several visits to fort Armstrong during the summer, and was always well treated. We were not as happy then in our village as formerly. Our people got more liquor than customary. I used all my influence to prevent drunkenness, but without effect. As the settlements progressed towards us, we became worse off, and more unhappy. Many of our people, instead of going to their old

[71] Here the editor inserted into the 1882 edition (p. 65) a long paragraph about a Sioux warrior and a Sauk maiden buried under a rock slide. He also added the following passage about Black Hawk's so-called watch tower:

"This tower to which my name had been applied, was a favorite resort and was frequently visited by me alone, when I could sit and smoke my pipe, and look with wonder and pleasure, at the grand scenes that were presented by the sun's rays, even across the mighty water. On one occasion a Frenchman, who had been making his home in our village, brought his violin with him to the tower, to play and dance for the amusement of a number of our people, who had assembled there, and while dancing with his back to the cliff, accidentally fell over it and was killed by the fall. The Indians say that always at the same time of the year, soft strains of the violin can be heard near the spot."

hunting grounds, where game was plenty, would go near to the settlements to hunt — and, instead of saving their skins to pay the trader for goods furnished them in the fall, would sell them to the settlers for whisky! and return in the spring with their families, almost naked, and without the means of getting any thing for them.

About this time my eldest son was taken sick and died. He had always been a dutiful child, and had just grown to manhood. Soon after, my youngest daughter, an interesting and affectionate child, died also. This was a hard stroke, because I loved my children. In my distress, I left the noise of the village, and built my lodge on a mound in my corn-field, and enclosed it with a fence, around which I planted corn and beans. Here I was with my family alone. I gave every thing I had away, and reduced myself to poverty. The only covering I retained, was a piece of buffalo robe. I resolved on blacking my face and fasting, for two years, for the loss of my two children — drinking only of water in the middle of the day, and eating sparingly of boiled corn at sunset. I fulfilled my promise, hoping that the Great Spirit would take pity on me.

My nation had now some difficulty with the Ioways, with whom we wished to be at peace. Our young men had repeatedly killed some of the Ioways; and these breaches had always been made up by giving presents to the relations of those killed. But the last council we had with them, we promised that, in case any more of their people were killed by ours, instead of presents, we would give up the person, or persons, that had done the injury. We made this determination known to our people; but, notwithstanding, one of our young men killed an Ioway the following winter.

A party of our people were about starting for the Ioway village to give the young man up. I agreed to accompany them. When we were ready to start, I called at the lodge for the young man to go with us. He was sick, but willing to go. His brother, however, prevented him, and insisted on going to die in his place, as he was unable to travel. We started, and on the seventh day arrived in sight of the Ioway village, and when within a short distance of it, halted and dismounted. We all bid farewell to our young brave, who entered the village alone, singing his *death-song*, and sat down in the square in the middle of the village. One of the Ioway chiefs came out to us. We told him that we had fulfilled our promise — that we had brought the brother of the young man who had killed one of their people — that he had volunteered to come in his place, in consequence of his brother being unable to travel from sickness. We had no further conversation, but mounted our horses and rode off. As we started, I cast my eye towards the village, and observed the Ioways coming out of their lodges with spears and war clubs. We took our trail back, and travelled until dark — then encamped and made a fire. We had not been here long, before we heard the sound of horses coming towards us. We seized our arms; but instead of an enemy, it was our young brave with two horses. He told me that after we had left him, they menaced him with death for some time — then gave him something to eat — smoked the pipe with him — and made him a present of the two horses and some goods, and started him after us. When we arrived at our village, our people were much pleased; and for the noble and generous conduct of the Ioways, on this occasion, not one of their people has been killed since by any of our nation.

That fall I visited Malden [72] with several of my band, and were well treated by our British father, who gave us a variety of presents. He also gave me a medal, and told me there never would be war between England and America again; but, for my fidelity to the British during the war that had terminated sometime before, requested me to come with my band every year and get presents, as Col. Dixon had promised me.

I returned, and hunted that winter on the Two-Rivers. The whites were now settling the country fast. I was out one day hunting in a bottom, and met three white men. They accused me of killing their hogs; I denied it; but they would not listen to me. One of them took my gun out of my hand and fired it off — then took out the flint, gave back my gun, and commenced beating me

[72] Fort Malden, a British stronghold at Amherstburg, Ontario, commanding the entrance to the Detroit River. It was the custom of the Sauk and other tribes to go once a year to Malden for presents — their reward for services to the British in wartime.

with sticks, and ordered me off. I was so much bruised that I could not sleep for several nights.

Some time after this occurrence, one of my camp cut a bee-tree, and carried the honey to his lodge. A party of white men soon followed, and told him that the bee-tree was theirs, and that he had no right to cut it. He pointed to the honey, and told them to take it; they were not satisfied with this, but took all the packs of skins that he had collected during the winter, to pay his trader and clothe his family with in the spring, and carried them off!

How could we like such people, who treated us so unjustly? We determined to break up our camp, for fear that they would do worse — and when we joined our people in the spring, a great many of them complained of similar treatment.

This summer our agent came to live at Rock Island. He treated us well, and gave us good advice. I visited him and the trader [73] very often during the summer, and, for the first time, heard talk of our having to leave my village. The trader explained to me the terms of the treaty that had been made, and said we would be obliged to leave the Illinois side of the Mississippi, and advised us to select a good place for our village, and remove to it in the spring. He pointed out the difficulties we would have to encounter, if we remained at our village on Rock river. He had great influence with the principal Fox chief, (his adopted brother,) and persuaded him to leave his village, and go to the west side of the Mississippi river, and build another — which he did the spring following.

Nothing was now talked of but leaving our village. Ke-o-kuck had been persuaded to consent to go; and was using all his influence, backed by the war chief at fort Armstrong, and our agent and trader at Rock Island, to induce others to go with him. He sent the crier through the village to inform our people that it was the wish

[73] George Davenport (1783–1845), who traded with the Indians after 1816, both independently and as a representative of the American Fur Company. He was an Englishman who had served in the War of 1812 (on the American side), and Gov. John Reynolds was later to appoint him acting quarter-master general with the rank of colonel in the Illinois militia. He was a founder, with Antoine LeClaire and others, of the city of Davenport, Iowa. In 1845 he was murdered in his home by a band of robbers.

of our Great Father that we should remove to the west side of the Mississippi — and recommended the Ioway river as a good place for the new village — and wished his party to make such arrangements, before they started out on their winter's hunt, as to preclude the necessity of their returning to the village in the spring.

The party opposed to removing, called upon me for my opinion. I gave it freely — and after questioning Quàsh-quà-me about the sale of the lands, he assured me that he "never had consented to the sale of our village." I now promised this party to be their leader, and raised the standard of opposition to Ke-o-kuck, with a full determination not to leave my village. I had an interview with Ke-o-kuck, to see if this difficulty could not be settled with our Great Father — and told him to propose to give other land, (any that our Great Father might choose, even our *lead mines*,) to be peaceably permitted to keep the small point of land on which our village and fields were situate. I was of opinion that the white people had plenty of land, and would never take our village from us. Ke-o-kuck promised to make an exchange if possible; and applied to our agent, and the great chief at St. Louis, (who has charge of all the agents,) for permission to go to Washington to see our Great Father for that purpose. This satisfied us for some time. We started to our hunting grounds, in good hopes that something would be done for us. During the winter, I received information that three families of whites had arrived at our village, and destroyed some of our lodges, and were making fences and dividing our corn-fields for their own use — *and were quarreling among themselves about their lines, in the division!* I immediately started for Rock river, a distance of ten day's travel, and on my arrival, found the report to be true. I went to my lodge, and saw a family occupying it. I wished to talk with them, but they could not understand me. I then went to Rock Island, and (the agent being absent,) told the interpreter what I wanted to say to those people, viz: "Not to settle on our lands — nor trouble our lodges or fences — that there was plenty of land in the country for them to settle upon — and they must leave our village, as we were coming back to it in the spring." The interpreter wrote me a paper, and I went back to the village, and showed it to the intruders, but could not understand their reply. I expected, however, that they would remove, as I requested them. I returned to Rock Island, passed the night there, and had a long conversation with the trader. He again advised me to give up, and make my village with Ke-o-kuck, on the Ioway river. I told him that I would not. The next morning I crossed the Mississippi, on very bad ice — but the Great Spirit made it strong, that I might pass over safe. I travelled three days farther to see the Winnebago sub-agent, and converse with him on the subject of our difficulties. He gave me no better news than the trader had done. I started then, by way of Rock river, to see the prophet, believing that he was a man of great knowledge.[74] When we met, I explained to him every thing as it was. He at once agreed that I was right, and advised me never to give up our village, for the whites to plough up the bones of our people. He said, that if we remained at our village, the whites would not trouble us — and advised me to get Ke-o-kuck, and the party that had consented to go with him to the Ioway in the spring, to return, and remain at our village.

I returned to my hunting ground, after an absence of one moon, and related what I had done. In a short time we came up to our village, and found that the whites had not left it — but that others had come, and that the greater part of our corn-fields had been enclosed. When we landed, the whites appeared displeased because

[74] The power that the Prophet wielded among the Sauk is shown by one Indian's assertion that he was head chief of the tribe. (Wee-sheet's testimony, Aug. 27, 1832, in Minutes of an Examination of Indian Prisoners, NA: AGO in IHI.) It is not likely that he could have been a principal chief, on a hereditary basis, since he was half Winnebago. But he was believed to be a man of great insight who was in contact with the spirit world. In this respect he was not unique, for many tribes in the first half of the nineteenth century had such prophets. Tecumseh, for example, was greatly influenced by his brother, a brave called the Shawnee Prophet.

The Prophet's village, 35 miles from the mouth of the Rock River, was so disreputable that Indian agent Joseph Street once recommended that it be burned. (Street to Cass, Aug. 26, 1831, IHI.) A year later it was destroyed by troops under Gen. Samuel Whiteside, pursuing Black Hawk. Street called the inhabitants of the village "renegadoes" and said they were generally disowned by other tribes. They consisted mainly of Winnebago from south of the Wisconsin River.

we had come back. We repaired the lodges that had been left standing, and built others. Ke-o-kuck came to the village; but his object was to persuade others to follow him to the Ioway. He had accomplished nothing towards making arrangements for us to remain, or to exchange other lands for our village. There was no more friendship existing between us. I looked upon him as a coward, and no brave, to abandon his village to be occupied by strangers. What *right* had these people to our village, and our fields, which the Great Spirit had given us to live upon?

My reason teaches me that *land cannot be sold*. The Great Spirit gave it to his children to live upon, and cultivate, as far as is necessary for their subsistence; and so long as they occupy and cultivate it, they have the right to the soil — but if they voluntarily leave it, then any other people have a right to settle upon it. Nothing can be sold, but such things as can be carried away.

In consequence of the improvements of the intruders on our fields, we found considerable difficulty to get ground to plant a little corn. Some of the whites permitted us to plant small patches in the fields they had fenced, keeping all the best ground for themselves. Our women had great difficulty in climbing their fences, (being unaccustomed to the kind,) and were ill-treated if they left a rail down.

One of my old friends thought he was safe. His corn-field was on a small island of Rock river. He planted his corn; it came up well — but the white man saw it! — he wanted the island, and took his team over, ploughed up the corn, and re-planted it for himself! The old man shed tears; not for himself, but the distress his family would be in if they raised no corn.

The white people brought whisky into our village, made our people drunk, and cheated them out of their horses, guns, and traps! This fraudulent system was carried to such an extent that I apprehended serious difficulties might take place, unless a stop was put to it. Consequently, I visited all the whites and begged them not to sell whisky to my people. One of them continued the practice openly. I took a party of my young men, went to his house, and took out his barrel and broke in the head and turned out the whisky.[75] I did this for fear some of the whites might be killed by my people when drunk.

Our people were treated badly by the whites on many occasions. At one time, a white man beat one of our women cruelly, for pulling a few suckers of corn out of his field, to suck, when hungry! At another time, one of our young men was beat with clubs by two white men for opening a fence which crossed our road, to take his horse through. His shoulder blade was broken, and his body badly bruised, from which he soon after *died!*[76]

Bad, and cruel, as our people were treated by the whites, not one of them was hurt or molested by any of my band. I hope this will prove that we are a peaceable people — having permitted ten men to take possession of our corn-fields; prevent us from planting corn; burn and destroy our lodges; ill-treat our women; and *beat to death* our men, without offering resistance to their barbarous cruelties. This is a lesson worthy for the white man to learn: to use forbearance when injured.

We acquainted our agent daily with our situation, and through him, the great chief at St. Louis — and hoped that something would be done for us. The whites were *complaining* at the same time that *we* were *intruding* upon *their rights!* THEY made themselves out the *injured* party, and *we* the *intruders!* and called loudly to the great war chief to protect *their* property!

How smooth must be the language of the whites, when they can make right look like wrong, and wrong like right.

During this summer, I happened at Rock Island, when a great chief arrived, (whom I had known as the great chief of Illinois, [governor Cole,] in company with another chief, who, I have been told, is a great writer, [judge Jas. Hall.] I called upon them and begged to explain to them the grievances under which me and my people were laboring, hoping that they could do something for us. The great chief, however, did not seem disposed to council

[75] At the cabin of Joshua Vandruff, one of the signers of a petition wherein the settlers asked Governor Reynolds for help in protecting their lives and property.
[76] A report that one of Black Hawk's sons had been tied and viciously beaten by white settlers is not mentioned by Black Hawk, and the incident probably did not occur. The story appeared in the *Kentucky Commonwealth*, May 28, 1833.

with me. He said he was no longer the great chief of Illinois — that his children had selected another father in his stead, and that he now only ranked as they did. I was surprised at this talk, as I had always heard that he was a good, brave, and great chief. But the white people never appear to be satisfied. When they get a good father, they hold councils, (at the suggestion of some bad, ambitious man, who wants the place himself,) and conclude, among themselves, that this man, or some other equally ambitious, would make a better father than they have, and nine times out of ten they don't get as good a one again.

I insisted on explaining to these two chiefs the true situation of my people. They gave their assent: I rose and made a speech, in which I explained to them the treaty made by Quàsh-quà-me, and three of our braves, according to the manner the trader and others had explained it to me. I then told them that Quàsh-quà-me and his party *denied*, positively, having ever sold my village; and that, as I had never known them to *lie*, I was determined to keep it in possession.

I told them that the white people had already entered our village, *burnt our lodges, destroyed our fences, ploughed up our corn, and beat our people:* that they had brought *whisky* into our country, *made our people drunk*, and taken from them their *horses, guns,* and *traps;* and that I had borne all this injury, without suffering any of my braves to raise a hand against the whites.

My object in holding this council, was to get the opinion of these two chiefs, as to the best course for me to pursue. I had appealed in vain, time after time, to our agent, who regularly represented our situation to the great chief at St. Louis, whose duty it was to call upon our Great Father to have justice done to us; but instead of this, we are told *that the white people want our country, and we must leave it to them!*

I did not think it possible that our Great Father wished us to leave our village, where we had lived so long, and where the bones of so many of our people had been laid. The great chief said that, as he was no longer a chief, he could do nothing for us; and felt sorry that it was not in his power to aid us — nor did he know how to advise us. Neither of them could do any thing for us; but both evidently appeared very sorry. It would give me great pleasure, at all times, to take these two chiefs by the hand.[77]

That fall I paid a visit to the agent, before we started to our hunting grounds, to hear if he had any good news for me. He had news! He said that the land on which our village stood was now ordered to be sold to individuals; and that, when sold, *our right* to remain, by treaty, would be at an end, and that if we returned next spring, we would be *forced* to remove!

We learned during the winter, that *part* of the lands where our village stood had been sold to individuals, and that the *trader* at Rock Island had bought the greater part that had been sold. The reason was now plain to me, why *he* urged us to remove. His object, we thought, was to get our lands. We held several councils that winter to determine what we should do, and resolved, in one of them, to return to our village in the spring, as usual; and concluded, that if we were removed by force, that the *trader*, agent, and others, must be the cause; and that, if found guilty of having us driven from our village, they should be *killed!* The trader stood foremost on this list. He had purchased the land on which my lodge stood, and that of our *grave yard* also! [78] Ne-a-pope promised to kill him, the agent, interpreter, the great chief at St. Louis, the war chief at fort Armstrong, Rock Island, and Ke-o-kuck — these being the principal persons to blame for endeavoring to remove us.[79]

Our women received bad accounts from the women that had been raising corn at the new village — the difficulty of breaking the new prairie with hoes — and the small quantity of corn raised. We were nearly in the same situation in regard to the latter, it being the first time I ever knew our people to be in want of provision.

[77] Of this council, James Hall later wrote: "He [Black Hawk] spoke of the intrusion upon their fields, the destruction of their growing corn, the ploughing up of the graves of their fathers, and the beating of their women; and added, 'we dare not resent any of these things. If we did, it would be said that the Indians were disturbing the white people, and troops would be sent out to destroy us.'" (McKenney and Hall, 72–73.)
[78] Davenport bought the site of Saukenuk and a large acreage of Indian farm lands in 1829. Keokuk's band left Saukenuk in the spring of 1829 but Black Hawk's band refused to go.
[79] In the 1882 edition the threat of murder is not attributed directly to Neapope, but reads, "We therefore proposed to kill him. . . ."

I prevailed upon some of Ke-o-kuck's band to return this spring to the Rock river village. Ke-o-kuck would not return with us. I hoped that we would get permission to go to Washington to settle our affairs with our Great Father. I visited the agent at Rock Island. He was displeased because we had returned to our village, and told me that we *must* remove to the west of the Mississippi. I told him plainly that we *would not!* I visited the interpreter at his house, who advised me to do as the agent had directed me. I then went to see the trader, and upbraided him for buying our lands. He said that if he had not purchased them, some person else would, and that if our Great Father would make an exchange with us, he would willingly give up the land he had purchased to the government. This I thought was fair, and began to think that he had not acted as badly as I had suspected. We again repaired our lodges, and built others, as most of our village had been burnt and destroyed. Our women selected small patches to plant corn, (where the whites had not taken them within their fences,) and worked hard to raise something for our children to subsist upon.

I was told that, according to the treaty, we had no *right* to remain upon the lands *sold,* and that the government would *force* us to leave them. There was but a small portion, however, that *had been sold;* the balance remaining in the hands of the government, we claimed the right (if we had no other) to "live and hunt upon, as long as it remained the property of the government," by a stipulation in the same treaty that required us to evacuate it *after* it had been sold. This was the land that we wished to inhabit, and thought we had the best right to occupy.

I heard that there was a great chief on the Wabash, and sent a party to get his advice. They informed him that we had not sold our village. He assured them then, that if we had not sold the land on which our village stood, our Great Father would not take it from us.

I started early to Malden to see the chief of my British Father, and told him my story. He gave the same reply that the chief on the Wabash had given; and in justice to him, I must say, that he never gave me any bad advice: but advised me to apply to our American Father, who, he said, would do us justice. I next called on the great chief at Detroit,[80] and made the same statement to him that I had to the chief of our British Father. He gave the same reply. He said, if we had not sold our lands, and would remain peaceably on them, that we would not be disturbed. This assured me that I was right, and determined me to hold out, as I had promised my people.

I returned from Malden late in the fall. My people were gone to their hunting ground, whither I followed. Here I learned that they had been badly treated all summer by the whites; and that a treaty had been held at Prairie du Chien. Ke-o-kuck and some of our people attended it, and found out that our Great Father had exchanged a small strip of the land that was ceded by Quàsh-quà-me and his party, with the Pottowatomies, for a portion of their land, near Chicago; and that the object of this treaty was to get it back again; and that the United States had agreed to give them *sixteen thousand dollars a year forever*, for this small strip of land — it being less than the twentieth part of that taken from our nation, for *one thousand dollars a year!* This bears evidence of something I cannot explain. This land, they say, belonged to the United States. What reason, then, could have induced them to exchange it with the Pottowatomies, if it was so valuable? Why not keep it? Or, if they found that they had made a bad bargain with the Pottowatomies, why not take back their land at a fair proportion of what they gave our nation for it? If this small portion of the land that they took from us for *one thousand dollars* a year, be worth *sixteen thousand dollars a year forever*, to the Pottowatomies, then the whole tract of country taken from us ought to be worth, to our nation, *twenty times* as much as this small fraction.

Here I was again puzzled to find out how the white people reasoned; and began to doubt whether they had any standard of right and wrong!

Communication was kept up between myself and the Prophet. Runners were sent to the Arkansas, Red river and Texas — not on the subject of our lands, but a secret mission, which I am not, at present, permitted to explain.

It was related to me, that the chiefs and headmen of the Foxes

[80] Lewis Cass, who was to become Secretary of War the following year.

had been invited to Prairie du Chien, to hold a council to settle the differences existing between them and the Sioux. That the chiefs and headmen, amounting to *nine*, started for the place designated, taking with them one woman — and were met by the Menomonees and Sioux, near the Ouisconsin, and all *killed*, except one man. Having understood that the whole matter was published shortly after it occurred, and is known to the white people, I will say no more about it.

I would here remark, that our pastimes and sports had been laid aside for the last two years. We were a divided people, forming two parties. Ke-o-kuck being at the head of one, willing to barter our rights merely for the good opinion of the whites; and cowardly enough to desert our village to them. I was at the head of the other party, and was determined to hold on to my village, although I had been *ordered* to leave it. But, I considered, as myself and band had no agency in selling our country — and that as provision had been made in the treaty, for us all to remain on it as long as it belonged to the United States, that we could not be *forced* away. I refused, therefore, to quit my village. It was here, that I was born — and here lie the bones of many friends and relations. For this spot I felt a sacred reverence, and never could consent to leave it, without being forced therefrom.

When I called to mind the scenes of my youth, and those of later days — and reflected that the theatre on which these were acted, had been so long the home of my fathers, who now slept on the hills around it, I could not bring my mind to consent to leave this country to the whites, for any earthly consideration.

The winter passed off in gloom. We made a bad hunt, for want of the guns, traps, &c. that the whites had taken from our people for whisky! The prospect before us was a bad one. I fasted, and called upon the Great Spirit to direct my steps to the right path. I was in great sorrow — because all the whites with whom I was acquainted, and had been on terms of friendship, advised me so contrary to my wishes, that I begun to doubt whether I had a *friend* among them.

Ke-o-kuck, who has a smooth tongue, and is a great speaker, was busy in persuading my band that I was wrong — and thereby making many of them dissatisfied with me. I had one consolation — for all the women were on my side, on account of their corn-fields.

On my arrival again at my village, with my band increased, I found it worse than before. I visited Rock Island. The agent again ordered me to quit my village. He said, that if we did not, troops would be sent to drive us off. He reasoned with me, and told me, it would be better for us to be with the rest of our people, so that we might avoid difficulty, and live in peace. The *interpreter* joined him, and gave me so many good reasons, that I almost wished I had not undertaken the difficult task that I had pledged myself to my brave band to perform. In this mood, I called upon the *trader*, who is fond of talking, and had long been my friend, but now amongst those advising me to give up my village. He received me very friendly, and went on to defend Ke-o-kuck in what he had done, and endeavored to show me that I was bringing distress on our women and children. He inquired, if some terms could not be made, that would be honorable to me, and satisfactory to my braves, for us to remove to the west side of the Mississippi? I replied, that if our Great Father would do us justice, and would make the proposition, I could then give up honorably. He asked me "if the great chief at St. Louis would give us six thousand dollars, to purchase provisions and other articles, if I would give up peaceably, and remove to the west side of the Mississippi?" After thinking some time, I agreed, that I could honorably give up, by being paid for it, according to our customs; but told him, that I could not make the proposal myself, even if I wished, because it would be dishonorable in me to do so.[81] He said he would do it, by sending word to the great chief at St. Louis, that he could remove us peaceably, for the amount stated, to the west side of the Mississippi. A steam boat arrived at the island during my stay. After its departure, the *trader* told me that he had "requested a war chief, who is stationed at Galena, and was on board of the steam boat, to

---

[81] This is a definite change of attitude. See above, p. 107, where he says, "I could not bring my mind to consent to leave this country to the whites, for any earthly consideration." Benjamin Drake (p. 198) says that Black Hawk's willingness to move for "six or eight thousand dollars" was brought to the attention of President Jackson and Secretary Cass.

make the offer to the great chief at St. Louis, and that he would soon be back, and bring his answer." I did not let my people know what had taken place, for fear they would be displeased. I did not much like what had been done myself, and tried to banish it from my mind.

After a few days had passed, the war chief returned, and brought for answer, that "the great chief at St. Louis would give us *nothing!* — and said if we did not remove immediately, we should be *drove off!*"

I was not much displeased with the answer brought by the war chief, because I would rather have laid my bones with my forefathers, than remove for any consideration. Yet if a friendly offer had been made, as I expected, I would, for the sake of my women and children, have removed peaceably.

I now resolved to remain in my village, and make no resistance, if the military came, but submit to my fate! I impressed the importance of this course on all my band, and directed them, in case the military came, not to raise an arm against them.

About this time, our agent was put out of office — for what reason, I never could ascertain.[82] I then thought, if it was for wanting to make us leave our village, it was right — because I was tired hearing him talk about it. The interpreter, who had been equally as bad in trying to persuade us to leave our village, was retained in office — and the young man who took the place of our agent, told the same old story over, about removing us. I was then satisfied, that this could not have been the cause.

Our women had planted a few patches of corn, which was growing finely, and promised a subsistence for our children — but the *white people again commenced ploughing it up!*

I now determined to put a stop to it, by clearing our country of the *intruders.* I went to the principal men and told them, that they

[82] Forsyth was removed from office in 1830 for no announced reason, and replaced by Felix St. Vrain. In a report on the causes of the Black Hawk War that he wrote on Oct. 1, 1832, Forsyth showed bitterness toward General Clark for his removal. "It is very well known . . . that if I had remained at Rocky Island as Indian agent no trouble would ever have taken place between the white people and the Indians . . . and no other person is to blame but Gen'l William Clark." (Draper mss., 9T54–59, in WHI.)

must and should leave our country — and gave them until the middle of the next day, to remove in. The worst left within the time appointed — but the one who remained, represented, that his family, (which was large,) would be in a starving condition, if he went and left his crop — and promised to behave well, if I would consent to let him remain until fall, in order to secure his crop. He spoke reasonably, and I consented.

We now resumed some of our games and pastimes — having been assured by the prophet that we would not be removed. But in a little while it was ascertained, that a great war chief, [Gen. Gaines,] [83] with a large number of soldiers, was on his way to Rock river. I again called upon the prophet, who requested a little time to see into the matter. Early next morning he came to me, and said he had been *dreaming!* "That he saw nothing bad in this great war chief, [Gen. Gaines,] who was now near Rock river. That the *object* of his mission was to *frighten* us from our village, that the white people might get our land for *nothing!*" He assured us that this "great war chief dare not, and would not, hurt any of us. That the Americans were at peace with the British, and when they made peace, the British required, (which the Americans agreed to,) that they should never interrupt any nation of Indians that was at peace — and that all we had to do to retain our village, was to *refuse* any, and every offer that might be made by this war chief."

The war chief arrived, and convened a council at the agency. Ke-o-kuck and Wà-pel-lo were sent for, and came with a number of their band. The council house was opened, and they were all admitted. Myself and band were then sent for to attend the council. When we arrived at the door, singing a *war song*, and armed with lances, spears, war clubs and bows and arrows, as if going to battle, I halted, and refused to enter — as I could see no necessity or propriety in having the room crowded with those who were already there. If the council was convened for us, why have others there in our room? The war chief having sent all out, except Ke-o-kuck, Wà-pel-lo, and a few of their chiefs and braves, we entered the council house, in this war-like appearance, being desirous to show the war

[83] Maj. Gen. Edmund P. Gaines (1777–1849), a hero of the War of 1812 and a soldier under Jackson in campaigns against the Creek and Seminole.

chief that we were *not afraid!* He then rose and made a speech.

He said:

"The president is very sorry to be put to the trouble and expense of sending a large body of soldiers here, to remove you from the lands you have long since ceded to the United States. Your Great Father has already warned you repeatedly, through your agent, to leave the country; and he is very sorry to find that you have disobeyed his orders. Your Great Father wishes you well; and asks nothing from you but what is reasonable and right. I hope you will consult your own interest, and leave the country you are occupying, and go to the other side of the Mississippi."

I replied: "That *we* had never sold our country. *We* never received any annuities from our American father! And *we* are determined to hold on to our village!" [84]

The war chief, apparently angry, rose and said: — "Who is *Black Hawk?* Who is *Black Hawk?*"

I responded:

"I am a *Sac!* my forefather was a SAC! and all the nations call me a SAC!!"

The war chief said:

"I came here, neither to *beg* nor *hire* you to leave your village.

---

[84] Here Black Hawk's editor italicized the word *we* for emphasis. If *we* means the Sauk and Fox, then the statement is completely false. But if it means Black Hawk's own band of followers, there is somewhat more justification for the claim.

That the Sauk and Fox did receive annuities is shown by scores of documents; and that they recognized them as payment for a land cession is shown in the complaint made by a delegation of chiefs in St. Louis, July, 1805. They said, "We have given away a great Country to Governor Wilkinson for a little thing . . . we made a bad bargain." (Wilkinson to Secretary of War, July 27, 1805, *Terr. Papers*, 13:168.) Wilkinson believed that the two tribes should receive larger annuities.

But Forsyth says that Black Hawk personally refused to accept any of the annuity goods after 1818 when he learned they were in payment for land. (Forsyth's report of Oct. 1, 1832, Draper mss., 9T54–59, in WHI.) Apparently he and many other Indians always believed the goods were gifts such as those they received from the British.

Coupled with Quashquame's frequent claim that he had never sold any land above the Rock River, this refusal to accept annuities may provide a basis for Black Hawk's insistence that "*we* had never sold our country. *We* never received any annuities from our American father!"

My business is to remove you, peaceably if I can, but *forcibly* if I must! I will now give you two days to remove in — and if you do not cross the Mississippi within that time, I will adopt measures to *force* you away!"

I told him that I never could consent to leave my village, and was determined not to leave it!

The council broke up, and the war chief retired to the fort. I consulted the prophet again: He said he had been dreaming, and that the Great Spirit had directed that a woman, the daughter of Mat-ta-tas, the old chief of the village, should take a stick in her hand and go before the war chief, and tell him that she is the daughter of Mat-ta-tas, and that he had always been the *white man's friend!* That he had fought their battles — been wounded in their service — and had always spoke well of them — and she had never heard him say that he had sold their village. The whites are numerous, and can take it from us if they choose; but she hoped they would not be so unfriendly. If they were, she had one favor to ask: she wished her people to be allowed to remain long enough to gather the provisions now growing in their fields: that she was a woman, and had worked hard to raise something to support her children! And, if we are driven from our village without being allowed to save our corn, many of our little children must perish with hunger!"

Accordingly, Ma-ta-tas' daughter was sent to the fort, accompanied by several of our young men. They were admitted. She went before the war chief, and told the story of the prophet! The war chief said that the president did not send him here to make treaties with the women, nor to hold council with them! That our young men must leave the fort, but she might remain if she wished!

All our plans were now defeated. We must cross the river, or return to our village and await the coming of the war chief with his soldiers. We determined on the latter: but finding that our agent, interpreter, trader, and Ke-o-kuck, (who were determined on breaking my ranks,) had seduced several of my warriors to cross the Mississippi, I sent a deputation to the agent, at the request of my band, pledging myself to leave the country in the fall, provided permission was given us to remain, and secure our crop of corn, then growing — as we would be in a starving situation if we were driven off without the means of subsistence.

The deputation returned with an answer from the war chief, "that no further time would be given us than that specified, and if we were not then gone, he would remove us!"

I directed my village crier to proclaim, that my orders were, in the event of the war chief coming to our village to remove us, that not a gun should be fired, nor any resistance offered. That if he determined to fight, for them to remain quietly in their lodges, and let him *kill them if he chose!*

I felt conscious that this great war chief would not hurt our people — and my object was not *war!* Had it been, we would have attacked, and killed the war chief and his braves, when in council with us — as they were then completely in our power.[85] But his manly conduct and soldierly deportment, his mild, yet energetic manner, which proved his bravery, forbade it.

Some of our young men who had been out as *spies*, came in and reported, that they had discovered a large body of mounted men coming towards our village, who looked like a *war party*.[86] They

[85] Of this meeting the General's aide-de-camp, George A. McCall, wrote: "We observed too that they were much more completely armed than is usual on such occasions; and many of them, indeed, had their bows bent, so unequivocal an indication of their hostile feeling, that it was thought proper privately to increase the guard. . . ." (George A. McCall to Archibald McCall, June 17, 1831, in McCall, 228.)

[86] An army of Illinois volunteers, called out by Gov. John Reynolds, had assembled at Beardstown, June 15, 1831, and were now marching on Black Hawk's village. General Gaines had at first told Reynolds, "I do not deem it necessary or proper to require militia," but after an unsatisfactory council with Black Hawk the General had accepted the offer of troops. There was no fighting this time, because Black Hawk moved his band across the river by night; the volunteers had to be content with burning the lodges at Saukenuk. (See Reynolds, chaps. 72 and 73, and the Gaines-Reynolds correspondence, Green and Alvord, 167–70.)

John Reynolds (1788–1865) was governor of Illinois from 1830 to 1834, and a key figure in the war. In calling out volunteers without a prior conference with General Gaines, and in repeatedly describing the presence of the Indian band as a hostile invasion, Reynolds did much to steer the War Department away from peaceful dealings with Black Hawk. It cannot be doubted, of course, that he was influenced by the apprehension of his frontier constituents. The fact that he associated a victory over the Indians with a political victory is indicated by a letter he wrote to General Atkinson at the beginning of the

arrived, and took a position below Rock river, for their place of encampment. The great war chief, (Gen. Gaines,) entered Rock river in a steam-boat, with his soldiers and one big gun! They passed, and returned close by our village; but excited no alarm among my braves. No attention was paid to the boat by any of our people — even our little children, who were playing on the bank of the river, as usual, continued their amusement. The water being shallow, the boat got aground, which gave the whites some trouble. If they had asked for assistance, there was not a brave in my band, who would not willingly, have aided them. Their people were permitted to pass and repass through our village, and were treated with friendship by our people.

The war chief appointed the next day to remove us! I would have remained and been taken prisoner by the *regulars*, but was afraid of the multitude of *pale faces*, who were on horseback, as they were under no restraint of their chiefs.

We crossed the Mississippi during the night, and encamped some distance below Rock Island.[87] The great war chief convened another council, for the purpose of making a treaty with us. In this treaty he agreed to give us corn in place of that we had left growing in our fields. I touched the goosequill to this treaty,[88] and was determined to live in peace.

The corn that had been given us, was soon found to be inadequate to our wants; when loud lamentations were heard in the camp, by our women and children, for their *roasting-ears, beans,* and *squashes.* To satisfy them, a small party of braves went over, in the night, to steal corn from their own fields. They were dis-

fighting in 1832. Apparently referring to the political situation in the state, he said, "Nothing will save me: but a descissive stroke on the Indians. I have so written to the War Dept. of the U. S. and so I write you." (April 22, 1832, IHI.)

87 "The appearance of the mounted Volunteers on the one side, & the regular troops with two pieces of Artillery on the other, aided by a Steam Boat armed with a piece of Artillery, & some Musquetry & Riflemen on the River induced the Indians to abandon the Village before the arrival of our Troops & without firing a Gun." (Gaines to Secretary of War, July 6, 1831, in Green and Alvord.)

88 It was not a treaty, but an "agreement and capitulation," that Black Hawk signed. It reaffirmed the treaties of 1804, 1816, and 1825, and provided that the Sauk would abandon all communication with the British.

covered by the whites, and fired upon. Complaints were again made of the depredations committed by some of my people, *on their own corn-fields!*

I understood from our agent, that there had been a provision made in one of our treaties for assistance in agriculture, and that we could have our fields ploughed, if we required it. I therefore called upon him, and requested him to have me a small log house built, and a field ploughed that fall, as I wished to live retired. He promised to have it done. I then went to the trader, and asked for permission to be buried in the grave-yard at our village, among my old friends and warriors; which he gave cheerfully. I then returned to my people satisfied.

A short time after this, a party of Foxes went up to Prairie du Chien to avenge the murder of their chiefs and relations, which had been committed the summer previous, by the Menomonees and Sioux. When they arrived in the vicinity of the encampment of the Menomonees, they met with a Winnebago, and inquired for the Menomonee camp; and requested him to go on before them and see if there were any Winnebagoes in it — and if so, to tell them that they had better return to their own camp. He went, and gave the information, not only to the Winnebagoes, but to the Menomonees, that they might be prepared. The party soon followed, killed twenty-eight Menomonees, and made their escape.

This retaliation, (which with us is considered lawful and right,) created considerable excitement among the whites! A demand was made for the Foxes to be surrendered to, and *tried* by, the white people! The principal men came to me during the fall, and asked my advice. I conceived that they had done right, and that our Great Father acted very *unjustly*, in demanding *them*, when he had suffered all their chiefs to be decoyed away, and *murdered* by the Menomonees, without having ever made a similar demand of *them*. If he had no right in the first instance, he had none now; and for my part, I conceive the *right* very *questionable*, if not altogether usurpation, in any case, where a difference exists between two nations, for him to interfere! The Foxes joined my band, with an intention to go out with them to hunt.

About this time, Ne-a-pope, (who started to Malden when it

was ascertained that the great war chief, Gen. Gaines, was coming to remove us,) returned. He said he had seen the chief of our British father, and asked him if the Americans could *force* us to leave our village? He said — "If we had not sold our village and land, the American government could not take them from us. That the *right*, being vested in us, could only be transferred by the voice and *will* of the whole nation; and that, as *we* had never given our consent to the sale of our country, it remained our exclusive property — from which the American government never could force us away! and that, in the event of *war*, we should have nothing to *fear!* as they would stand by and *assist* us!"

He said he had called at the prophet's village on his way down, and had there learned, for the first time, that we had left our village. He informed me, privately, that the prophet was anxious to see me, as he had much good news to tell me, and that I would hear good news in the spring from our British father. The prophet requested me to inform you of all the particulars. I would much rather, however, you should see him, and learn all from himself. But I will tell you, that he has received expresses from our British father, who says that he is going to send us guns, ammunition, provisions, and clothing, early in the spring. The vessels that bring them will come by way of Mil-wá-ke. The prophet has likewise received wampum and tobacco from the different nations on the lakes — Ottowas, Chippewas, Pottowatomies; and as for the Winnebagoes, he has them all at his command. We are going to be happy once more!

I told him that I was pleased to hear that our British father intended to see us righted. That we had been driven from our lands without receiving any thing for them — and I now began to hope, from his *talk*, that my people would be once more happy. If I could accomplish this, I would be satisfied. I am now growing old, and could spend the remnant of my time anywhere. But I wish first to see my people happy. I can then leave them cheerfully. This has always been my constant aim; and I now begin to hope that our sky will soon be clear.

Ne-a-pope said: "The prophet told me that all the different tribes before mentioned would *fight* for us, if necessary, and the

British would support us. And, if we *should be whipped,* (which is hardly possible,) we will still be safe, the prophet having received a friendly *talk* from the chief of Wàs-sa-cum-mi-co, (at Selkirk's settlement,) [89] telling him, that if we were not satisfied in our country, to let him know, and he would make us happy. That he had received information from our British father, that we had been badly treated by the Americans. We must go and see the prophet. I will go first; you had better remain and get as many of our people to join us as you can. You now know every thing that we have done. We leave the matter with you to arrange among your people as you please. I will return to the prophet's village to-morrow; you can, in the mean time, make up your mind as to the course you will take, and send word to the prophet by me, as he is anxious to assist us, and wishes to know whether you will join us, and assist to make your people happy!"

During that night, I thought over everything that Ne-a-pope had told me, and was pleased to think that, by a little exertion on my part, I could accomplish the object of all my wishes. I determined to follow the advice of the prophet, and sent word by Ne-a-pope, that I would get all my braves together, and explain every thing that I had heard to them; and recruit as many as I could from the different villages.

Accordingly, I sent word to Ke-o-kuck's band and the Fox tribe, and explained to them all the good news I had heard. They would not hear. Ke-o-kuck said that I had been imposed upon by *liars,* and had much better remain where I was and keep quiet. When he found that I was determined to make an attempt to secure my village, and fearing that some difficulty would arise, he made application to the agent and great chief at St. Louis, for permission for the chiefs of our nation to go to Washington to see our Great Father, that we might have our difficulties settled amicably. Ke-o-kuck also requested the trader, who was going on to Washington, to call on our Great Father and explain every thing to him, and ask for permission for us to come on and see him.

Having heard nothing favorable from the great chief at St. Louis,

[89] The Fifth Earl of Selkirk (Thomas Douglas, 1770–1820) had established a Scottish colony near the present city of Winnipeg, Canada, in 1811.

I concluded that I had better keep my band together, and recruit as many more as possible, so that I would be prepared to make the attempt to rescue my village in the spring, provided our Great Father did not send word for us to go to Washington.

The trader returned. He said he had called on our Great Father and made a full statement to him in relation to our difficulties, and had asked leave for us to go to Washington, but had received no answer.

I had determined to listen to the advice of my friends — and if permitted to go to see our Great Father, to abide by his counsel, whatever it might be. Every overture was made by Ke-o-kuck to prevent difficulty, and I anxiously hoped that something would be done for my people, that it might be avoided. But there was *bad management somewhere, or the difficulty that has taken place would have been avoided.*

When it was ascertained that we would not be permitted to go to Washington, I resolved upon my course, and again tried to recruit some braves from Ke-o-kuck's band to accompany me, but could not.

Conceiving that the *peaceable disposition* of Ke-o-kuck and his people had been, in a great measure, the cause of our having been driven from our village, I ascribed their present feelings to the same cause; and immediately went to work to recruit all my own band, and made preparations to ascend Rock river. I made my encampment on the Mississippi, where fort Madison had stood; requested my people to rendezvous at that place, and sent out soldiers to bring in the warriors, and stationed my sentinels in a position to prevent any from moving up until *all* were ready.

My party having all come in and got ready, we commenced our march up the Mississippi — our women and children in canoes, carrying such provisions as we had, camp equipage, &c. and my braves and warriors on horseback, armed and equipped for defence.[90] The prophet came down and joined us below Rock river,

[90] Black Hawk crossed the Mississippi near the mouth of the lower Iowa on April 5, 1832. The commonly accepted date of April 6 probably arises from an error in an early published version of the crossing. Atkinson's letterbook in the files of the Illinois State Historical Library gives the date as April 5.

having called at Rock Island, on his way down, to consult the war chief, agent, and trader, who (he said) used many arguments to dissuade him from going with us; and requested him to come and meet us, and turn us back. They told him also, that there was a war chief on his way to Rock Island with a large body of soldiers.

The prophet said he would not listen to this *talk*, because no war chief dare molest us as long as we are at *peace*. That we had a right to go where we pleased peaceably; and advised me to say nothing to my braves and warriors until we encamped that night. We moved onward until we arrived at the place where Gen. Gaines had made his encampment the year before, and encamped for the night. The prophet then addressed my braves and warriors. He told them to "follow us, and act like braves, and we had nothing to *fear*, but much to *gain*. That the American war chief might come, but would not, nor dare not, interfere with us so long as we acted peaceably! That we were not *yet ready* to act otherwise. We must wait until we ascend Rock river and receive our reinforcements, and we will then be able to withstand any army!" [91]

That night the *White Beaver*, [Gen. Atkinson,] with a party of soldiers, passed up in steam boats. Our party became alarmed, expecting to meet the soldiers at Rock river, to prevent us from going up. On our arrival at its mouth, we discovered that the steam boats had passed on. I was fearful that the war chief had stationed his men on some bluff, or in some ravine, that we might be taken by surprise. Consequently, on entering Rock river, we commenced beating our drums and singing, to show the Americans that we were not afraid.

Having met with no opposition, we moved up Rock river leisurely some distance, when we were overtaken by an express from the White Beaver, with an ORDER for me to return with my band, and recross the Mississippi again. I sent him word that "I would

[91] In an interview with Maj. John Bliss at this time, the Prophet admitted inviting Black Hawk across the river to plant corn. He was surly on this occasion, as shown by Major Bliss's account:

"Question: Then you do not care much if they do get into war.

"Answer: I have nothing to say; if you think so, you can make war, those (the Sacs) are my young men, I can call on them, and the Wenebagoes, I am half Sac, & half Wenebago." (St. Vrain to Clark, April 6, 1832, NA:AGO in IHI.)

not (not recognizing his *right* to make such a demand,) as I was acting peaceably, and intended to go to the prophet's village, at his request, to make corn."

The express returned. We moved on, and encamped some distance below the prophet's village. Here another express came from the White Beaver, threatening to pursue us and *drive* us back, if we did not return peaceably! This message roused the spirit of my band, and all were determined to remain with me and contest the ground with the war chief, should he come and attempt to drive us. We therefore directed the express to say to the war chief, "if he wished to *fight* us, he might come on!" We were determined never to be driven, and equally so, *not to make the first attack*, our object being to act only on the defensive. This we conceived our right.

Soon after the express returned, Mr. Gratiot,[92] sub-agent for the Winnebagoes, with several of the chiefs and headmen of the Winnebago nation, came to our encampment. He had no interpreter — and was compelled to talk through his chiefs. They said the object of his mission was, to persuade us to return. But they advised us to go on — assuring us, that the further we went up Rock river, the more friends we would meet, and our situation be bettered: that they were on our side, and all their people were our friends: that we must not give up — but continue to ascend Rock river, on which, in a short time, we would receive a reinforcement sufficiently strong to repulse any enemy! They said they would go down with their agent, to ascertain the strength of the enemy, and then return and give us the news: that they had to use some stratagem to *deceive* their agent, in order to *help* us!

During this council, a number of my braves hoisted the British flag, mounted their horses, and surrounded the council lodge! I discovered that the agent was very much frightened! I told one of his chiefs to tell him that he need not be alarmed — and then went out and directed my braves to desist. Every warrior immediately

[92] Henry Gratiot (1789–1836), owner of a mining and smelting works at Gratiot's Grove, in what is now Lafayette County, Wis. He was the son of Charles Gratiot, a St. Louis fur trader, and the brother of Gen. Charles Gratiot, Jr., chief engineer of the United States Army.

dismounted, and returned to his lodge. After the council adjourned, I placed a sentinel at the agent's lodge, to guard him — fearing that some of my warriors might again frighten him! I had always thought that he was a good man, and was determined that he should not be hurt. He started, with his chiefs, for Rock Island.[93]

Having ascertained that the White Beaver would not permit us to remain here, I began to consider what was best to be done, and concluded to keep up the river and see the Pottowatomies, and have a talk with them. Several Winnebago chiefs were present, whom I advised of my intentions, as *they* did not seem disposed to render us any assistance. I asked them if they had not sent us *wampum* during the winter, and requested us to come and join their people and enjoy all the rights and privileges of their country? They did not deny this; and said if the white people did not interfere, they had no objection to our making corn this year, with our friend the prophet; but did not wish us to go any further up.[94]

The next day, I started with my party to Kish-wá-co-kee.[95] That night I encamped a short distance above the prophet's village. After all was quiet in my camp, I sent for my chiefs, and told them that we had been *deceived!* That all the fair promises that had been

[93] One message that General Atkinson sent to Black Hawk said, in part, "if you do not come back and go on the other side of the great river I shall write to your great father & tell him of your bad conduct. You will be sorry if you do not came back. . . . If your hearts are good I will send an officer to talk with you in three or four days." (Atkinson to Black Hawk, April 24, 1832, IHI.)
When the Indians met in council to discuss Atkinson's ultimatum, Black Hawk was inclined to shift the responsibility. He said, "I do not command the Indians. The Village belongs to the Chiefs. Why do they want to know my feelings. I have no bad feelings. My opinion goes with my Chiefs. I will follow them up the Rock River, and my braves are all of the same mind." (Black Hawk to Atkinson, April 26, 1832, IHI.) That was the report brought back by Indian messengers sent to carry Atkinson's letter. But when Black Hawk later addressed a message directly to Atkinson via Henry Gratiot, he was more forceful. He sent word that his heart was "bad," and that he would fight any force sent against him. (Atkinson to Macomb, April 27, 1832, IHI.)
[94] The Winnebago were not united in their attitude toward Black Hawk's campaign. Many of those living south of the Wisconsin River were aiding him, but most of those north of the river were opposed to his activities. (Street to Scott, Aug. 22, and Scott to Cass, Aug. 19, 1832, NA:SW in IHI.)
[95] The Kishwaukee River, which joins the Rock River below Rockford, Ill. In Black Hawk's day the white settlers called it Sycamore Creek.

held out to us, through Ne-a-pope, were *false!* But it would not do
to let our party know it. We must keep it secret among ourselves —
and move on to Kish-wá-co-kee, as if all was right, and say something on the way to encourage our people. I will then call on the
Pottowatomies, and hear what they say, and see what they will do.

We started the next morning, after telling our people that news
had just come from Mil-wâ-kee, that a chief of our British father
would be there in a few days!

Finding that all our plans were defeated, I told the prophet that
he must go with me, and we would see what could be done with
the Pottowatomies. On our arrival at Kish-wá-co-kee, an express
was sent to the Pottowatomie villages. The next day a deputation
arrived. I inquired if they had corn in their villages? They said they
had very little, and could not spare any! I asked them different
questions, and received unsatisfactory answers. This talk was in
the presence of all my people. I afterwards spoke to them privately,
and requested them to come to my lodge after my people had got to
sleep. They came, and took seats. I asked them if they had received
any news from the lake from the British? They said, no. I inquired
if they had heard that a chief of our British father was coming
to Mil-wâ-kee, to bring us guns, ammunition, goods and provisions? They said, no! I then told them what news had been brought
to me, and requested them to return to their village, and tell the
chiefs that I wished to see them and have a talk with them.

After this depuation started, I concluded to tell my people, that
if the White Beaver came after us, we would go back — as it was
useless to think of stopping or going on without provisions. I discovered that the Winnebagoes and Pottowatomies were not disposed to render us any assistance. The next day, the Pottowattomie
chiefs arrived at my camp. I had a dog killed, and made a feast.
When it was ready, I spread my *medicine bags*, and the chiefs began to eat. When the ceremony was about ending, I received news,
that three or four hundred white men, on horseback, had been seen
about eight miles off. I immediately started three young men, with
a white flag, to meet them, and conduct them to our camp, that we
might hold a council with them, and descend Rock river again.
And directed them, in case the whites had *encamped*, to return,

and I would go and see *them*. After this party had started, I sent five young men to see what might take place. The first party went to the encampment of the whites, and were taken prisoners. The last party had not proceeded far, before they saw about twenty men coming towards them in full gallop? [96] They stopped, and finding that the whites were coming so fast, in a warlike attitude, they turned and retreated, but were pursued, and two of them overtaken and *killed!* The others made their escape. When they came in with the news, I was preparing my *flags* to meet the war chief. The alarm was given. Nearly all my young men were absent, about ten miles off. I started with what I had left, (about *forty,*) and had proceeded but a short distance, before we saw a part of the army approaching. I raised a yell, and said to my braves: — "Some of our people have been killed! — wantonly and cruelly murdered! We must revenge their death!"

In a little while we discovered the whole army coming towards us in full gallop! We were now confident that our first party had been killed! I immediately placed my men in front of some bushes, that we might have the first fire, when they approached close enough. They made a halt some distance from us. I gave another yell, and ordered my brave warriors to *charge* upon them — expecting that we would all be killed! They did charge! Every man rushed and fired, and the enemy *retreated!* in the utmost confusion and consternation, before my little, but brave band of warriors!

After pursuing the enemy some distance, I found it useless to follow them, as they rode so fast, and returned to my encampment with a few of my braves, (about *twenty-five* having gone in pursuit of the enemy.) I lighted my pipe, and sat down to thank the Great Spirit for what we had done. I had not been long meditating, when two of the three young men I had sent out with the flag to meet the American war chief, entered! My astonishment was not greater than my joy to see them living and well. I eagerly listened to their story, which was as follows:

"When we arrived near to the encampment of the whites, a number of them rushed out to meet us, bringing their guns with them. They took us into their camp, where an American, who

---

[96] The question mark was changed to an exclamation in later editions.

spoke the Sac language a little, told us that his chief wanted to know how we were — where we were going — where our camp was — and where Black Hawk was? We told him that we had come to see his chief; that our chief had directed us to conduct him to our camp, in case he had not encamped; and, in that event, to tell him, that he [Black Hawk,] would come to see him; he wished to hold a council with him, as he had given up all intenton of going to war.[97]

"At the conclusion of this talk, a party of white men came in, on horseback. We saw by their countenances that something had happened. A general tumult arose. They looked at us with indignation — talked among themselves for a moment — when several cocked their guns — in a second, they fired at us in the crowd; our companion fell dead! We rushed through the crowd and made our escape. We remained in ambush but a short time, before we heard yelling, like Indians running an enemy. In a little while we saw some of the whites in full speed. One of them came near us. I threw my tomahawk, and struck him on the head, which brought him to the ground! I ran to him, and *with his own knife, took off his scalp!* I took his gun, mounted his horse, and took my friend here behind me. We turned to follow our braves, who were running the enemy, and had not gone far before we overtook a white man, whose horse had mired in a swamp! My friend alighted, and tomahawked the man, who was apparently fast under his horse! He took his *scalp*, horse, and *gun!* By this time our party was some

---

[97] After this paragraph, in the 1882 edition, Black Hawk described an incident in which he recognized a captured American prisoner as one who had been an adopted member of his tribe in years past (see above, p. 69). The man was bound to a tree, and Black Hawk, in recognition of past friendship, set him free. This incident does not appear in any edition of the autobiography published during Black Hawk's lifetime. The wording is similar to an account of the experiences of Elijah Kilbourn which first appeared in the *Soldiers' Cabinet*, Philadelphia, 1855.

Kilbourn's story contained many incredible details. He said he was forced to live at Saukenuk for three years — yet the many traders, interpreters, and agents who were in the area would certainly have known of him if he had been there. He says he was captured and bound to a tree after the Battle of Stillman's Run, but no other version of the battle verifies his statement. He said that Black Hawk spoke to him in "good English." If the old Indian could have spoken good English he would not have needed the constant services of an interpreter when dealing with the Americans and the British; his knowledge of English was slight.

distance ahead. We followed on, and saw several white men lying dead on the way. After riding about six miles, we met our party returning. We asked them how many of our men had been killed? They said none, after the Americans retreated. We inquired then, how many whites had been killed? They replied, that they did not know; but said we will soon ascertain, as we must *scalp* them as we go back. On our return, we found *ten men*, besides the *two* we had killed before we joined our friends. Seeing that they did not yet recognise us, it being dark, we again asked, how many of our braves had been killed? They said *five!* We asked, who they were? They replied that the first party of three, who went out to meet the American war chief, had all been taken prisoners, and killed in the encampment; and that out of a party of five, who followed to see the meeting of the first party and the whites, *two* had been killed! We were now certain that they did not recognise us — nor did we tell them *who we were* until we arrived at our camp! The news of our death had reached it some time before, and all were surprised to see us again!"

The next morning I told the crier of my village to give notice that we must go and bury our dead. In a little while all were ready. A small deputation was sent for our absent warriors, and the remainder started. We first disposed of our dead, and then commenced an examination, in the enemy's deserted encampment, for plunder. We found arms, ammunition, and provisions, all which we were in want of — particularly the latter, as we were entirely without. We found, also, a variety of *saddle-bags*, (which I distributed among my braves,) and a small quantity of *whisky!* and some *little* barrels that *had* contained this *bad medicine;* but they were *empty!* I was surprised to find that the whites carried whisky with them, as I had understood that all the *pale faces* belonged to the *temperance societies!*

The enemy's encampment was in a skirt of woods near a run, about half a day's travel from Dixon's ferry. We attacked them in the prairie, with a few bushes between us, about sundown, and I expected that my whole party would be killed! I never was so much surprised, in all the fighting I have seen — knowing, too, that the Americans, generally, shoot well — as I was to see this army of

several hundreds, *retreating!* WITHOUT SHOWING FIGHT!! and passing immediately through their encampment. I did think that they
intended to halt here, as the situation would have forbidden attack
by *my party*, if *their number* had not exceeded *half mine!* as we
would have been compelled to take the *open prairie*, whilst they
could have *picked trees* to shield themselves from our fire!

Never was I so much surprised in my life, as I was in this attack!
An army of three or four hundred, after having learned that we
were sueing for *peace*, to attempt to kill the flag-bearers that had
gone, unarmed, to ask for a meeting of the war chiefs of the two
contending parties to hold a council, that I might return to the
west side of the Mississippi, to come forward, with a full determination to demolish the few braves I had with me, to *retreat*, when they
had *ten* to *one*, was unaccountable to me. It proved a different spirit from any I had ever before seen among the *pale faces!* I expected
to see them fight as the Americans did with the *British* during the
last war! — but they had no such braves among them! [98]

I had resolved upon giving up the war — and sent a *flag of peace*

[98] Little can be added to Black Hawk's tale of the encounter at Sycamore
Creek, except to identify the American troops involved and add a few statistics.

The battle occurred May 14, 1832, a few miles southwest of the mouth of
Sycamore Creek in present Ogle County, Ill. The site of the battle immediately
became known to the army as Stillman's Run. Maj. Isaiah Stillman, with a
battalion of militia, was preparing to encamp at sundown when the Indians
appeared with the flag of truce. The Black Hawk War might have ended at this
moment, had the Stillman camp been better organized and the men better
disciplined. Instead, the flag was not taken seriously and the little group of
Indians watching from a distance, to see how the trucebearers fared, were
assumed to be hostile.

Governor Reynolds later wrote, "Judging from all I can discover in the
premises, I believe the number of warriors were between fifty and sixty."
(Reynolds, 234.) Gen. Samuel Whiteside told Atkinson that Stillman had about
260 men. (Letter of May 18, 1832, in IHI.) Reynolds said he had about 275.
Twelve of Stillman's men were lost in the skirmish.

After his capture many weeks later, Neapope said, "I had a white flag to
shake hands, and we did not think of fighting the Americans if we met them."
(Minutes of an Examination of Indian Prisoners, Aug. 20, 1832, NA:AGO in IHI.)

Stillman's "run" received special mention in Atkinson's report of Nov. 19,
1832, to the Adjutant General, in which he attempted to explain some of the
difficulties of the campaign: "My plan, which had been strongly inculcated of
not striking a blow until it could be done with a certainty of success was destroyed by the precipitate movement of Stillmans Battalion."

to the American war chief — expecting, as a matter of right, reason and justice, that our *flag would be respected*, (I have always seen it so in war among the whites,) and a council convened, that we might explain our grievances, having been driven from our village the year before, without being permitted to gather the corn and provisions which our women had labored hard to cultivate, and ask for permission to return — thereby giving up all idea of going to war against the whites.

Yet, instead of this *honorable course* which *I* have always practised in war, I was *forced* into WAR, with about *five hundred* warriors, to contend against *three* or *four thousand!*

The *supplies* that Ne-a-pope and the prophet told us about, and the reinforcements we were to have, were never heard of; (and it is but justice to our British father to say, *were never promised — his chief having sent word in lieu of the lies that were brought to me*, "FOR US TO REMAIN AT PEACE, AS WE COULD ACCOMPLISH NOTHING BUT OUR OWN RUIN, BY GOING TO WAR!")

What was now to be done? It was worse than folly to turn back and meet an enemy where the odds was so much against us — and thereby sacrifice ourselves, our wives and children, to the fury of an enemy who had *murdered* some of our brave and *unarmed* warriors, when they were on a mission to *sue for peace!*

Having returned to our encampment, and found that all our young men had come in, I sent out *spies*, to watch the movement of the army, and commenced moving up Kish-wá-co-kee, with the balance of my people. I did not know where to go to find a place of safety for my women and children, but expected to find a good harbor about the head of Rock river. I concluded to go there — and thought my best route would be to go round the head of Kish-wá-co-kee, so that the Americans would have some difficulty, if they attempted to follow us.

On arriving at the head of Kish-wá-co-kee, I was met by a party of Winnebagoes, who seemed to rejoice at our success. They said they had come to offer their services, and were anxious to join us. I asked them if they knew where there was a safe place for my women and children. They told me that they would send two old men with us to guide us to a good and safe place.

I arranged war parties to send out in different directions, before I proceeded further. The Winnebagoes went alone. The war parties having all been fitted out and started, we commenced moving to the *Four Lakes*, the place where our guides were to conduct us. We had not gone far, before six Winnebagoes came in with *one scalp!* They said they had killed a man at a grove, on the road from Dixon's to the lead mines.[99] Four days after, the party of Winnebagoes who had gone out from the head of Kish-wá-co-kee, overtook us, and told me that they had killed four men, and taken their scalps; and that one of them was Ke-o-kuck's father, (the agent.) [100] They proposed to have a dance over their scalps! I told them that I could have no dancing in my camp, in consequence of my having lost three young braves; but they might dance in their own camp — which they did.

Two days after, we arrived in safety at the place where the Winnebagoes had directed us. In a few days a great number of our warriors came in. I called them all around me, and addressed them. I told them, "Now is the time, if any of you wish to come into distinction, and be honored with the medicine bag! Now is the time to show your courage and bravery, and avenge the murder of our three braves!"

Several small parties went out, and returned again in a few days, with success — bringing in provision for our people. In the mean time, some *spies* came in, and reported that the army had fallen back to Dixon's ferry; and others brought news that the horsemen had broken up their camp, disbanded, and returned home.[101]

[99] The man was William Durley, killed near Polo, Ill., May 19, 1832. He was one of a party of six militiamen carrying dispatches from Galena to Atkinson's camp at Dixon's Ferry.

[100] Felix St. Vrain, who had replaced Forsyth at the Indian agency on Rock Island. He had been sent by Atkinson with messages from Dixon's Ferry to Rock Island, by way of Galena. With him were six frontier settlers. In the attack near Kellogg's Grove, St. Vrain and three others were killed; the rest escaped.

[101] The mounted volunteers recruited by Governor Reynolds, and commanded by General Whiteside, clamored to be discharged. When the officers voted on whether to continue pursuing the Indians or to leave the field, the vote was a tie. General Whiteside then swore he would never lead them, even if someone

Finding that all was safe, I made a *dog feast*, preparatory to leaving my camp with a large party, (as the enemy were stationed so far off.) Before my braves commenced feasting, I took my *medicine bags*, and addressed them in the following language:

"*Braves and Warriors:* — These are the medicine bags of our forefather, Muk-a-tà-quet, who was the father of the Sac nation. They were handed down to the great war chief of our nation, Nà-ma-kee, who has been at war with all the nations of the lakes and all the nations of the plains, and have never yet been disgraced! I expect you all to protect them!"

After the ceremony was over, and our feasting done, I started with about two hundred warriors, following my great medicine bags! I directed my course towards sunset, and dreamed, the second night after we started, that there was a great feast for us after one day's travel! I told my warriors my dream in the morning, and we all started for Mos-co-ho-co-y-nak, [Apple river.] When we arrived in the vicinity of a fort the white people had built there, we saw four men on horseback. One of my braves fired and wounded a man, when the others set up a yell, as if a large force were near and ready to come against us. We concealed ourselves, and remained in this position for some time, watching to see the enemy approach — but none came. The four men, in the mean time, ran to the fort and gave the alarm. We followed them, and attacked their fort! [102] One of their braves, who seemed more

changed a vote to break the tie; Reynolds then decided to discharge the men. (Reynolds, 372–76.)

The troops were discharged at Ottawa, except for about 250 men who volunteered to stay another twenty days and protect the frontier. The campaign could not proceed until a new levy of volunteers could gather at Fort Deposit, fifteen miles below Ottawa. General Atkinson was then able to take the field with a force of 3,000 regulars and 400 volunteers. But because of sickness, unfit horses, etc., among the volunteers, their number had dwindled to 900 by the end of the campaign. (Atkinson to the Adjutant General, Nov. 19, 1832, IHI.)

William Cullen Bryant was traveling in Illinois while the second levy was assembling. He wrote to his wife, June 19, "every few miles on our way we fell in with bodies of Illinois militia . . . a hard-looking set of men, unkempt and unshaved, wearing shirts of dark calico and sometimes calico capotes." (Godwin, ed., II, 20.)

[102] The Apple River Fort a few miles southeast of Galena. Even before the appearance of this war party, the citizens of the isolated lead-mining area of

valiant than the rest, raised his head above the picketing to fire at us, when one of my braves, with a well-directed shot, put an end to his bravery! Finding that these people could not all be killed, without setting fire to their houses and fort, I thought it more prudent to be content with what flour, provisions, cattle and horses we could find, than to set fire to their buildings, as the light would be seen at a distance, and the army might suppose that we were in the neighborhood, and come upon us with a force too strong. Accordingly, we opened a house and filled our bags with flour and provisions — took several horses, and drove off some of their cattle.

We started in a direction towards sunrise. After marching a considerable time, I discovered some white men coming towards us. I told my braves that we would get into the woods and kill them when they approached. We concealed ourselves until they came near enough, and then commenced yelling and firing, and made a rush upon them. About this time, their chief, with a party of men, rushed up to rescue the men we had fired upon. In a little while they commenced retreating, and left their chief and a few braves, who seemed willing and anxious to fight! They acted like *braves*, but were forced to give way when I rushed upon them with my braves. In a short time the chief returned with a larger party. He seemed determined to fight, and anxious for a battle. When he came near enough, I raised the yell, and firing commenced from both sides. The chief (who seemed to be a small man) addressed his warriors in a loud voice; but they soon retreated, leaving him and a few braves on the battle-field. A great number of my warriors pursued the retreating party, and killed a number of their horses as they ran. The chief and his few braves were unwilling to leave the field. I ordered my braves to rush upon them, and had the mortification of seeing two of my *chiefs* killed, before the enemy retreated.

Galena had been in a state of fear and confusion. Zachary Taylor wrote to Atkinson, "Our difficulties thicken on us daily, the people of Galena are perfectly panic struck." And Lucius Lyon reported, "Women and children are rushing in from all parts of the country to go off in Steam Boats." (Taylor to Atkinson, June 1, 1832, IHI; and *Terr. Papers*, 12:478.)

This young chief deserves great praise for his courage and bravery; but, fortunately for us, his army was not all composed of such brave men! [103]

During this attack, we killed several men and about forty horses, and lost two young chiefs and seven warriors. My braves were anxious to pursue them to the fort, attack, and burn it. But I told them that it was useless to waste our powder, as there was no possible chance of success if we did attack them — and that, as we had run the bear into his hole, we would there leave him, and return to our camp.

On arriving at our encampment, we found that several parties of our *spies* had returned, bringing intelligence that the army had commenced moving. Another party of *five* came in and said they had been pursued for several hours, and were attacked by twenty-five or thirty whites in the woods; that the whites rushed in upon them, as they lay concealed, and received their fire, without seeing them. They immediately retreated, whilst we reloaded. They entered the thicket again, and as soon as they came near enough, we fired! Again they retreated, and again they rushed into the thicket and fired! We returned their fire, and a skirmish ensued between two of their men and one of ours, who was killed by having his throat cut! This was the only man we lost. The enemy having had three killed, they again retreated.[104]

Another party of three Sacs had come in, and brought in two young white squaws, whom they had given to the Winnebagoes, to

[103] The young chief was Maj. John Dement and the occasion was the Battle of Kellogg's Grove, June 25, 1832. Black Hawk's account coincides broadly with a manuscript narrative, endorsed by Dement, in the files of the Illinois State Historical Library. (Also see above, pp. 28–29.)

[104] In present Stephenson County, about twelve miles east of Kellogg's Grove, Capt. James W. Stephenson with about eighteen men engaged in this game of hide-and-seek with the Indians on June 18. After rushing the thicket three times, Stephenson withdrew. A more famous battle had occurred two days before, at the Pecatonica River, when Col. Henry Dodge and twenty-nine men engaged a party of seventeen Indians and killed them all. The fighting was violent though the numbers were small, and the Indians were protected by a six-foot bank of earth. Considering the fact that four of Dodge's men were holding horses, four were scouting, and three were wounded early, the opposing forces were rather evenly matched. (Stevens, 182–83.)

take to the whites. They said they had joined a party of Pottowatomies, and went with them as a war party, against the settlers on
the Illinois.

The leader of this party, a Pottowatomie, had been severely
whipped by this settler, some time before, and was anxious to
avenge the insult and injury. While the party was preparing to
start, a young Pottowatomie went to the settler's house, and told
him to leave it — that a war party was coming to murder them.[105]
They started, but soon returned again, as it appeared that they
were all there when the war party arrived! The Pottowatomies
killed the whole family, except two young squaws, whom the Sacs
took up on their horses, and carried off, to save their lives. — They
were brought to our encampment, and a messenger sent to the
Winnebagoes, as they were *friendly on both sides*, to come and get
them, and carry them to the whites. If these young men belonging
to my band, had not gone with the Pottowatomies, the two young
squaws would have shared the same fate as their friends.[106]

During our encampment at the Four Lakes, we were hard put
to, to obtain enough to eat to support nature. Situate in a swampy,
marshy country, (which had been selected in consequence of the

[105] When a war party endangered the settlers, Shabona or Shaubena rode about
the valley to spread the word, accompanied by his son and nephew. Shabona
was a Potawatomi chief who, with Waubonsee and others, had been entertained at dog feasts by Black Hawk and invited to join the crusade. Instead,
they and about ninety other Potawatomi joined the Americans to oppose
Black Hawk. Most of them were discharged July 22 before the actual fighting
began. Until then they had served as guides, spies, and expresses. (See muster
roll of Potawatomi in U. S. service, in IHI.)
[106] This is Black Hawk's account of the Indian Creek massacre and the capture
of Rachel and Sylvia Hall. William Davis, a settler on Indian Creek about
twelve miles north of Ottawa, had quarreled with a band of Potawatomi about
a dam he had built across the creek. They claimed it interfered with their
fishing.

The settlers were attacked on May 20, 1832, at the Davis home, and fifteen
persons were killed. It is apparently true that the Hall girls were taken by the
Sauk Indians in the war party. They were then turned over to the Winnebago,
held for eleven days without mistreatment, and released. (See the statement of
Rachel Hall, in George E. Walker to Atkinson, Oct. 10, 1834, IHI.) A Sauk chief
named Ioway testified after his capture that the Winnebago had promised the
Sauk captors corn, sugar, and a horse in return for the girls, but that the
promise was not kept. (Ioway's testimony, Minutes of an Examination of Indian Prisoners, Aug. 27, 1832, NA:AGO in IHI.)

great difficulty required to gain access thereto,) there was but little game of any sort to be found — and fish were equally scarce. The great distance to any settlement, and the impossibility of bringing supplies therefrom, if any could have been obtained, deterred our young men from making further attempts. We were forced to dig *roots* and *bark trees*, to obtain something to satisfy hunger and keep us alive! Several of our old people became so much reduced, as actually to *die with hunger!* And, finding that the army had commenced moving, and fearing that they might come upon and surround our encampment, I concluded to remove my women and children across the Mississippi, that they might return to the Sac nation again. Accordingly, on the next day, we commenced moving, with five Winnebagoes acting as our guides, intending to descend the Ouisconsin.[107]

[107] General Atkinson, pursuing Black Hawk, decided at about this time to dismiss some of the volunteer companies not attached to larger units. He mustered them out in mid-July and sent them back down toward Dixon's Ferry. One of the men sent back was a private named Abraham Lincoln.

Lincoln had enlisted April 21 at New Salem, where he was a clerk in Denton Offutt's store, and had been elected captain of a company in the Fourth Regiment, Whiteside's Brigade. After a month of service his company had been discharged and he had re-enlisted for another twenty days — this time remaining a private in another company. His company had marched to Galena in search of Indians, then back to Dixon's Ferry, then to Fort Deposit. When his second enlistment had expired he had re-enlisted for thirty more days as a private in an independent spy company. With this unit he had marched to Kellogg's Grove the day after Major Dement's battle, then back again to Dixon's Ferry. He had gone as far north as the Lake Koshkonong country before he was mustered out.

After his discharge Lincoln returned once more to Dixon's Ferry and continued on to Peoria, where he bought a canoe and paddled it down the Illinois River to Havana. From there he walked overland to New Salem. When he read in a back issue of the *Sangamo Journal* a list of Sangamon County candidates for office who had served in the militia, and did not find himself listed although he was running for the Illinois legislature, he asked the publisher to print a correction. The issue of July 19 carried this statement: "Some weeks ago we gave a list of those candidates of this County (omitting by accident the name of Captain Lincoln, of New Salem,) who were on the frontier periling their lives in the service of their country."

Reflecting on his service in the war, Lincoln wrote to Jesse W. Fell in 1859, "I was elected a Captain of Volunteers — a success which gave me more pleasure than any I have had since."

A paymaster's receipt roll in the General Accounting Office, NA (photostat in IHI), shows that Lincoln earned $26.15 during the three weeks of his first re-

Ne-a-pope, with a party of twenty, remained in our rear, to watch for the enemy, whilst we were proceeding to the Ouisconsin, with our women and children. We arrived, and had commenced crossing them to an island, when we discovered a large body of the enemy coming towards us. We were now compelled to fight, or sacrifice our wives and children to the fury of the whites! I met them with fifty warriors, (having left the balance to assist our women and children in crossing,) about a mile from the river, when an attack immediately commenced. I was mounted on a fine horse, and was pleased to see my warriors so brave. I addressed them in a loud voice, telling them to stand their ground, and never yield it to the enemy. At this time I was on the rise of a hill, where I wished to form my warriors, that we might have some advantage over the whites. But the enemy succeeded in gaining this point, which compelled us to fall back into a deep ravine, from which we continued firing at them and they at us, until it began to grow dark. My horse having been wounded twice during this engagement, and fearing from his loss of blood, that he would soon give out — and finding that the enemy would not come near enough to receive our fire, in the dusk of the evening — and knowing that our women and children had had sufficient time to reach the island in the Ouisconsin, I ordered my warriors to return, in different routes, and meet me at the Ouisconsin — and were astonished to find that the enemy were not disposed to pursue us.

In this skirmish, with fifty braves, I defended and accomplished my passage over the Ouisconsin, with a loss of only SIX men; though opposed by a host of mounted militia.[108]

enlistment as a private. This included base pay of $6.66 a month plus allowances for travel, for supplying his own horse and arms, etc.

For a detailed account of Lincoln's service, see Harry E. Pratt's summary in *Lincoln, 1809–1839*, a volume in the *Lincoln Day by Day* series.

[108] The number of Indian casualties at the Battle of Wisconsin Heights is unknown. Black Hawk says he lost six men. Two Sauk chiefs testified, in the minutes of an examination of Indian prisoners, Aug. 27, 1832, that five men were killed in battle; but one of the chiefs said that other men died of wounds on the way to the Mississippi. (NA:AGO in IHI.) And a squaw who escaped down the Wisconsin reported that sixty-eight Indians were killed. (Loomis to Atkinson, July 30, 1832, in IHI.)

Colonel Dodge's version, in a letter written the day after the battle: "Our loss was one man killed and eight wounded; from the scalps taken by the

I would not have fought there, but to gain time for my women and children to cross to an island. A warrior will duly appreciate the embarrassments I labored under — and whatever may be the sentiments of the *white people*, in relation to this battle, my nation, though fallen, will award to me the reputation of a great brave, in conducting it.

The loss of the enemy could not be ascertained by our party; but I am of opinion, that it was much greater, in proportion, than mine. We returned to the Ouisconsin, and crossed over to our people.[109]

Here some of my people left me, and descended the Ouisconsin, hoping to escape to the west side of the Mississippi, that they might return home. I had no objection to their leaving me, as my people were all in a desperate condition — being worn out with travelling, and starving from hunger. Our only hope to save ourselves, was to get across the Mississippi.[110] But few of this party escaped. Unfor-

Winnebagoes as well as those taken by the Whites and Indians carried from the field of Battle we must have killed about 40 of them. . . ." (Dodge to Loomis, July 22, 1832, IHI.)

[109] Many years later, Jefferson Davis termed this crossing the most brilliant exhibition of military tactics he had ever witnessed. He said that during the battle the Indian women tore bark from the trees upon which to float their papooses across, while the men fought against superior numbers with bravery and desperation. Speaking of an event long past, Davis recalled the scene as if he had been an eye-witness. (Aldrich, 408–9.) But see Scanlan for evidence that Davis saw no combat against Black Hawk. According to Scanlan, he was on leave from March through July, 1832, and returned to duty only in time to escort Black Hawk and other prisoners from Fort Crawford to Jefferson Barracks.

[110] The troops had no thought of letting Black Hawk reach the Mississippi. Atkinson, in a letter to General Alexander, spoke of the need to "stop the enemy and bring him to Action before he crosses the Mississippi. . . ." (June 26, 1832, IHI.) And Colonel Dodge, writing to Atkinson, said, "Be assured every possible exertion will Be made to destroy the Enemy crippled as they must be with their wounded and families as well as their want of provision supplies." (July 24, 1832, IHI.)

In pursing Black Hawk after he had obviously taken flight, Atkinson was acting under orders of President Jackson. General Macomb had written on May 22 that the President wished Black Hawk as a prisoner. And he had added: "It is firmly believed that unless energetic measures are taken at this time with Black Hawk and his band, the same outrages on the frontiers of Illinois will be repeated annually to the great annoyance and disquiet of the frontier settle-

tunately for them, a party of soldiers from Prairie du Chien, was stationed on the Ouisconsin, a short distance from its mouth, who fired upon our distressed people. Some were killed, others drowned, several taken prisoners, and the balance escaped to the woods and perished with hunger. Among this party were a great many women and children.[111]

I was astonished to find that Ne-a-pope and his party of *spies* had not yet come in — they having been left in my rear to bring the news, if the enemy were discovered. It appeared, however, that the whites had come in a different direction, and intercepted our trail but a short distance from the place where we first saw them — leaving our spies considerably in the rear. Ne-a-pope, and one other, retired to the Winnebago village, and there remained during the war! The balance of his party, being *brave men*, and considering our interest as their own, returned, and joined our ranks.

Myself and band having no means to descend the Ouisconsin, I started, over a rugged country, to go to the Mississippi, intending to cross it, and return to my nation. Many of our people were compelled to go on foot, for want of horses, which, in consequence of their having had nothing to eat for a long time, caused our march to be very slow. At length we arrived at the Mississippi, having lost some of our old men and little children, who perished on the way with hunger.[112]

ments, attended with endless expense to the United States." (Macomb to Atkinson, IHI.)

The President re-emphasized this position on June 12 by writing a note to the Acting Secretary of War, John Robb, saying that "the Black Hawk & his party must be chastized and a speedy & honorable termination put to this war, which will hereafter deter others from the like unprovoked hostilities by Indians on our frontier." (Endorsement on letter from Robb to Atkinson, June 12, NA:AGO in IHI.) Robb sent this word on to Atkinson.

[111] The detachment of regulars at the mouth of the Wisconsin, commanded by Lt. Joseph Ritner, had been sent out from Fort Crawford. Some of the Indians who escaped them and scattered into the woods were wiped out by an expedition of Menominee, under Col. Samuel Stambaugh, who had been recruited from the Green Bay, Wis., area.

[112] "The prisoners are the most miserable looking poor creatures you can imagine. Wasted to mere skeletons, clothed in rags scarcely sufficient to hide their nakedness, some of the children look as if they had starved so long they could not be restored." (Street to Clark, Aug. 1, 1832, NA:OIA in IHI.)

We had been here but a little while, before we saw a steam boat (the "Warrior,") coming. I told my braves not to shoot, as I intended going on board, so that we might save our women and children. I knew the captain, [THROCKMORTON,] and was determined to give myself up to him. I then sent for my *white flag*.[113] While the messenger was gone, I took a small piece of white cotton, and put it on a pole, and called to the captain of the boat, and told him to send his little canoe ashore, and let me come on board. The people on the boat asked whether we were Sacs or Winnebagoes. I told a Winnebago to tell them that we were Sacs, and wanted to give ourselves up! A Winnebago on the boat called to us *"to run and hide, that the whites were going to shoot!"* About this time one of my braves had jumped into the river, bearing a white flag to the boat — when another sprang in after him, and brought him to shore. The firing then commenced from the boat, which was returned by my braves, and continued for some time. Very few of my people were hurt after the first fire, having succeeded in getting behind old logs and trees, which shielded them from the enemy's fire.

The Winnebago, on the steam boat, must either have misunderstood what was told, or did not tell it to the captain correctly; because I am confident that he would not have fired upon us, if he had known my wishes. I have always considered him a good man, and too great a brave to fire upon an enemy when sueing for quarters.[114]

---

[113] "Black Hawk said to the women, 'run and get me the white flag. I will go on board that boat.' He told the men to put down their guns, and the women got behind trees." (Testimony of Kishkasshoi, Aug. 19, 1832, NA:SW in IHI.) The Indians had also displayed a white flag unsuccessfully at Stillman's Run.

[114] The *Warrior* opened fire on the Indians, believing that their flag of truce was a hoax. Throckmorton later claimed to have killed twenty-three. He returned next day to continue the battle. (Armstrong, 468, 472; Holmes to Atkinson, Aug. 5, 1832, IHI.) Joseph Throckmorton had devoted four years to steamboating on the upper Mississippi and owned the 111-foot vessel in partnership with William Hempstead, of Galena. It was new on the river, having been launched in mid-summer at Pittsburgh.

When the Indians were encountered, the steamer was returning downstream from Wabashaw's village, now Wabasha, Minn., "to git the Scioux to watch the Shores of the river that the Hos. Indians, men do not cross with impunity — the boat has a 6 Pr. [pounder] on board." (Loomis to Atkinson, July 30–31, 1832, IHI.)

After the boat left us, I told my people to cross, if they could, and wished: that I intended going into the Chippewa country. Some commenced crossing, and such as had determined to follow them, remained — only three lodges going with me. Next morning, at daybreak, a young man overtook me, and said that all my party had determined to cross the Mississippi — that a number had already got over safe, and that he had heard the white army last night within a few miles of them. I now began to fear that the whites would come up with my people, and kill them, before they could get across. I had determined to go and join the Chippewas; but reflecting that by this I could only save myself, I concluded to return, and die with my people, if the Great Spirit would not give us another victory! During our stay in the thicket, a party of whites came close by us, but passed on without discovering us!

Early in the morning a party of whites, being in advance of the army, came upon our people, who were attempting to cross the Mississippi. They tried to give themselves up — the whites paid no attention to their entreaties — but commenced *slaughtering* them! In a little while the whole army arrived. Our braves, but few in number, finding that the enemy paid no regard to age or sex, and seeing that they were murdering helpless women and little children, determined to *fight until they were killed!* As many women as could, commenced swimming the Mississippi, with their children on their backs. A number of them were drowned, and some shot, before they could reach the opposite shore.[115]

[115] Gen. Winfield Scott later apologized to the Indians for killing women and children, explaining that "some of them, in the different battles, were in the bushes and high grass, with their warriors, and were hurt or killed unavoidably, infinitely to the regret of our warriors. . . ." (NA, Records of the U. S. Senate, 22nd Cong., in ICC.) The genuine regret of the soldiers is indicated by Wakefield (p. 88) who participated in the battle: "If they [the women and children] had shown themselves, they would have come off much better, but fear prevented them; and in their retreat, trying to hide from us, many of them were killed . . . but not intentionally by any man . . . we all well knew the squaws and children could do us no harm, and could not help what the old Black Hawk and other chiefs did."

There are conflicting reports about the number of casualties at the Battle of the Bad Axe. Atkinson reported to Scott that U. S. losses totaled six killed, eighteen wounded; Indian losses, 150 men killed. (Aug. 5, 1832, IHI.) Weesheet, a Sauk chief, testified that 200 men, women, and children escaped across

One of my braves, who gave me this information, piled up some saddles before him, (when the fight commenced,) to shield himself from the enemy's fire, and killed three white men! But seeing that the whites were coming too close to him, he crawled to the bank of the river, without being perceived, and hid himself under it, until the enemy retired. He then came to me and told me what had been done. After hearing this sorrowful news, I started, with my little party, to the Winnebago village at Prairie La Cross.[116] On my arrival there, I entered the lodge of one of the chiefs, and told him that I wished him to go with me to his father — that I intended to give myself up to the American war chief, and *die*, if the Great Spirit saw proper! He said he would go with me. I then took my *medicine bag*, and addressed the chief. I told him that it was "the soul of the Sac nation — that it never had been dishonored in any battle — take it, it is my life — dearer than life — and give it to the American chief!" He said he would keep it, and take care of it, and if I was suffered to live, he would send it to me.

During my stay at the village, the squaws made me a white dress of deer skin. I then started, with several Winnebagoes, and went to their agent, at Prairie du Chien, and gave myself up.[117]

the Mississippi. (Minutes of an Examination of Indian Prisoners, Aug. 27, 1832, NA:AGO in IHI.)

Agent Joseph M. Street wrote to William Clark, "The Inds. were pushed litterally into the Mississippi, the current of which was at one time perceptibly tinged with the blood of the Indians who were shot on its margin & in the stream. . . . It is impossible to say how many Inds. have been killed, as most of them were shot in the water or drowned in attempting to cross the Mississippi." (Aug. 3, 1832, NA:OIA in IHI.)

According to Ellen Whitney, working from contemporary documents in the Illinois State Historical Library, the estimates of Indian casualties throughout the campaign vary from 442 to 592. A large portion of these casualties occurred at the Bad Axe and during the later attack by the Sioux.

Reporting to President Jackson on the successful completion of the campaign, General Macomb emphasized retribution. He said that the Indians had undoubtedly been chastised for crossing the Mississippi, and that vengeance had now been inflicted upon the murderers of the Menominee. (Aug. 11, 1832, typed copy in CHI.)

[116] "None of us liked the Prophet and Black Hawk leaving as they did. — We said 'now they have brought us to ruin and lost us our women and children, then have run to save their own lives.' " (Wee-sheet's testimony, Aug. 27, 1832.)

[117] As a reward for bringing Black Hawk in, the Winnebago were promised twenty horses and one hundred dollars. And General Scott promised to speak

On my arrival there, I found to my sorrow, that a large body of Sioux had pursued, and killed, a number of our women and children, who had got safely across the Mississippi. The whites ought not to have permitted such conduct — and none but *cowards* would ever have been guilty of such cruelty — which has always been practised on our nation by the Sioux.[118]

The massacre, which terminated the war, lasted about two hours. Our loss in killed, was about sixty, besides a number that were drowned. The loss of the enemy could not be ascertained by my braves, exactly; but they think that they killed about *sixteen*, during the action.

I was now given up by the agent to the commanding officer [119] at fort Crawford, (the White Beaver having gone down the river.) We remained here a short time, and then started to Jefferson Barracks, in a steam boat, under the charge of a young war chief, [Lieut. Jefferson Davis] who treated us all with much kindness. He is a good and brave young chief, with whose conduct I was much pleased.[120] On our way down, we called at Galena, and remained a short time. The people crowded to the boat to see us; but the war chief would not permit them to enter the apartment where we were — knowing, from what his own feelings would have been, if he had been placed in a similar situation, that we did not wish to have a gaping crowd around us.

of their good conduct to the Great Father in Washington. (Scott to Cass, Sept. 9, 1832, NA:AGO in IHI.)

[118] The Sioux attacked the survivors about a week after the crossing, 120 miles from the Mississippi near the trading post at the Red Cedar River. The 100 Sioux warriors inflicted heavy losses on the straggling band, and Agent Street told them they were now redeemed, in the eyes of the government, for an earlier failure to serve the U. S. as warriors. (Street to Scott, Aug. 22, 1832, NA:AGO in IHI.) A treaty of peace between the Sioux and the Sauk and Fox, signed Aug. 19, 1825, at Prairie du Chien, had failed to put down old rivalries. The text is in Kappler, II, 250.

[119] Col. Zachary Taylor.

[120] Also detailed to accompany the prisoners was Lt. Robert Anderson, of the Third Regiment Artillery, who had been Assistant Inspector General of the troops in the field. The records show that Anderson, upon leaving Fort Crawford, received from the quartermaster's stores a pair of handcuffs, a ball and chain, and a shackle. (Memo of Sept. 3, 1832, in IHI.) Anderson wrote many years later that he and Davis both escorted Black Hawk down the river. (*Wis. Hist. Coll.*, 10:172.)

We passed Rock Island, without stopping. The great war chief, [Gen. Scott,] who was then at fort Armstrong, came out in a small boat to see us; but the captain of the steam boat would not allow any body from the fort to come on board of his boat, in consequence of the cholera raging among the soldiers.[121] I did think that the captain ought to have permitted the war chief to come on board to see me, because I could see no danger to be apprehended by it. The war chief looked well, and, I have since heard, was constantly among his soldiers, who were sick and dying, administering to their wants, and had not caught the disease from them — and I thought it absurd to think that any of the people on the steam boat, could be afraid of catching the disease from a *well* man. But these people have not got bravery like war chiefs, who never *fear* any thing! [122]

On our way down, I surveyed the country that had cost us so much trouble, anxiety, and blood, and that now caused me to be a prisoner of war. I reflected upon the ingratitude of the whites, when I saw their fine houses, rich harvests, and every thing desirable around them; and recollected that all this land had been ours, for which me and my people had never received a dollar, and

[121] See pp. 20–21 for General Macomb's account of Scott's difficulties with cholera. One of the Illinois citizens who died during an epedemic the next year was Ninian Edwards, former governor.

Scott wrote to Cass, "The master of the boat would not allow me to board him, although Black Hawk said he had important disclosures to make which he would make only to me. It is understood that those disclosures related to the Winnebagoes of the Rock River, and their conduct in the late war." (Sept. 9, 1832, NA:AGO in IHI.) Black Hawk had also confided to Joseph Street that he had disclosures to make, according to a report in the *Galenian*, Sept. 5. Apparently he decided not to complain about his allies, for General Atkinson later wrote to Scott, "The Black Hawk denies having any disclosures to make. The Prophet makes none, both equivocate, when questioned, upon all points connected with their own conduct or that of their associates." (Sept. 16, IHI.)

[122] A few days after Black Hawk passed down the river, a treaty was signed by the United States and the defeated Indians (see Appendix 2, p. 161). The treaty council had been delayed by cholera. The disease was disappearing when the Indians began to arrive at Rock Island, but as a precaution against infection they were not allowed within Fort Armstrong. Two of the council sessions were held on the west bank of the river in what is now Iowa, but the third session, at which the treaty was signed, convened on Rock Island. By this time, Sept. 21, the cholera had abated. (NA, Records of the U. S. Senate, 22nd Cong., in ICC.)

that the whites were not satisfied until they took our village and our grave-yards from us, and removed us across the Mississippi.

On our arrival at Jefferson barracks, we met the great war chief, [White Beaver,] who had commanded the American army against my little band. I felt the humiliation of my situation: a little while before, I had been the leader of my braves, now I was a prisoner of war! but had surrendered myself. He received us kindly, and treated us well.

We were now confined to the barracks, and forced to wear the *ball and chain!* This was extremely mortifying, and altogether useless. Was the White Beaver afraid that I would break out of his barracks, and run away? Or was he ordered to inflict this punishment upon me? If I had taken him prisoner on the field of battle, I would not have wounded his feelings so much, by such treatment — knowing that a brave war chief would prefer *death* to *dishonor!* But I do not blame the White Beaver for the course he pursued — it is the custom among white soldiers, and, I suppose, was a part of his duty.[123]

The time dragged heavily and gloomy along throughout the winter, although the White Beaver done every thing in his power to render us comfortable. Having been accustomed, throughout a long life, to roam the forests o'er — to go and come at liberty — confinement, and under such circumstances, could not be less than torture!

We passed away the time making pipes, until spring, when we were visited by the agent, trader, and interpreter, from Rock Island, Ke-o-kuck, and several chiefs and braves of our nation, and

[123] "I still retain the Prophet and Napope in irons," wrote General Atkinson to the President in December, "the others having been more or less afflicted with cholera their bands were removed & have not been replaced." Atkinson enclosed a plea from Black Hawk and the Prophet that they be set free. They had asked that their words be sent to their Great Father. Black Hawk's message included a business proposition: ". . . that the President may take pity on the women & children & that they may be safe hereafter & the prisoners restored to their nation, we will willingly give up the lead mines on the Mississippi." (He was unaware that the mines already had been ceded.) The Prophet's message was apologetic: "I have the reputation of communing with the Great Spirit, but I am only a common man, I am not worse than other men, I have given advice to my own people, but only for their benefit & to the detriment of none. . . ." (Atkinson to Jackson, Dec. 28, 1832, NA:AGO in IHI.)

my wife and daughter. I was rejoiced to see the two latter, and spent my time very agreeably with them and my people, as long as they remained.

The trader presented me with some dried venison, which had been killed and cured by some of my friends. This was a valuable present; and although he had given me many before, none ever pleased me so much. This was the first meat I had eaten for a long time, that reminded me of the former pleasures of my own wigwam, which had always been stored with plenty.

Ke-o-kuck and his chiefs, during their stay at the barracks, petitioned our Great Father, the President, to release us; and pledged themselves for our good conduct. I now began to hope that I would soon be restored to liberty, and the enjoyment of my family and friends; having heard that Ke-o-kuck stood high in the estimation of our Great Father, because he did not join me in the war. But I was soon disappointed in my hopes. An order came from our Great Father to the White Beaver, to send us on to Washington.

In a little while all were ready, and left Jefferson barracks on board of a steam boat, under charge of a young war chief, whom the White Beaver sent along as a guide to Washington.[124] He carried with him an interpreter and one soldier. On our way up the Ohio, we passed several large villages, the names of which were explained to me. The first is called Louisville, and is a very pretty

---

[124] Here, in the 1882 edition, are inserted the following sentences: "We were accompanied by Keokuk, wife and son, Appanooce, Wapello, Poweshiek, Pashippaho, Nashashuk, Saukee, Musquaukee, and our interpreter. Our principal traders, Col. George Davenport, of Rock Island, and S. S. Phelps and clerk, William Cousland, of the Yellow Banks, also accompanied us."

According to the letters exchanged between Jefferson Barracks and Washington, the only persons who accompanied the six prisoners were an officer, two non-commissioned officers, and an interpreter. There is no possibility that Keokuk was present, since he had at that time been asking permission to go to Washington, and his request had been refused. (Herring to Clark, May 4, 1833, NA:OIA.) The commissioned officer, referred to in the correspondence as Lt. Alexander, was probably Lt. T. L. Alexander of the Sixth Infantry. The interpreter, referred to as Mr. St. Vrain, was probably Charles St. Vrain, brother of Felix.

More information about Black Hawk's trip to the East Coast will be found in the Introduction, pp. 1–15, including excerpts from Maj. John Garland's official report.

village, situate on the bank of the Ohio river. The next is Cincinnati, which stands on the bank of the same river. This is a large and beautiful village, and seemed to be in a thriving condition. The people gathered on the bank as we passed, in great crowds, apparently anxious to see us.

On our arrival at Wheeling, the streets and river's banks were crowded with people, who flocked from every direction to see us. While we remained here, many called upon us, and treated us with kindness — no one offering to molest or misuse us. This village is not so large as either of those before mentioned, but is quite a pretty village.

We left the steam boat here, having travelled a long distance on the prettiest river (except our Mississippi,) that I ever saw — and took the stage. Being unaccustomed to this mode of travelling, we soon got tired, and wished ourselves seated in a canoe on one of our own rivers, that we might return to our friends. We had travelled but a short distance, before our carriage turned over, from which I received a slight injury, and the soldier had one arm broken. I was sorry for this accident, as the young man had behaved well.

We had a rough and mountainous country for several days, but had a good trail for our carriage. It is astonishing to see what labor and pains the white people have had to make this road, as it passes over an immense number of mountains, which are generally covered with rocks and timber; yet it has been made smooth, and easy to travel upon.[125]

Rough and mountainous as is this country, there are many wigwams and small villages standing on the road side. I could see nothing in the country to induce the people to live in it; and was astonished to find so many whites living on the hills!

I have often thought of them since my return to my own people; and am happy to think that they prefer living in their *own* country, to coming out to *ours*, and driving us from it, that they might live upon and enjoy it — as many of the whites have already done. I think, with them, that wherever the Great Spirit places his peo-

[125] The Cumberland Road or National Road, first highway built with federal funds.

ple, they ought to be satisfied to remain, and thankful for what He has given them; and not drive others from the country He has given them, because it happens to be better than theirs! This is contrary to our way of thinking; and from my intercourse with the whites, I have learned that one great principle of *their religion* is, "to do unto others as you wish them to do unto you!" Those people in the mountains seem to act upon this principle; but the settlers on our frontiers and on our lands, seem never to think of it, if we are to judge by their actions.

The first village of importance that we came to, after leaving the mountains, is called Hagerstown. It is a large village to be so far from a river, and is very pretty. The people appear to live well, and enjoy themselves much.

We passed through several small villages on the way to Fredericktown, but I have forgotten their names. This last is a large and beautiful village. The people treated us well, as they did at all the other villages where we stopped.

Here we came to another road, much more wonderful than that through the mountains. They call it a *rail road!* I examined it carefully, but need not describe it, as the whites know all about it. It is the most astonishing sight I ever saw. The great road over the mountains will bear no comparison to it — although it has given the white people much trouble to make. I was surprised to see so much labor and money expended to make a good road for easy travelling. I prefer riding on horseback, however, to any other way; but suppose that these people would not have gone to so much trouble and expense to make a road, if they did not prefer riding in their new fashioned carriages, which seem to run without any trouble. They certainly deserve great praise for their industry.

On our arrival at Washington, we called to see our Great Father, the President. He looks as if he had seen as many winters as I have, and seems to be a *great brave!* I had very little talk with him, as he appeared to be busy, and did not seem much disposed to talk. I think he is a good man; and although he talked but little, he treated us very well. His wigwam is well furnished with every thing good and pretty, and is very strongly built.

He said he wished to know the *cause* of my going to war against his white children. I thought he ought to have known this before; and, consequently, said but little to him about it — as I expected he knew as well as I could tell him.

He said he wanted us to go to fortress Monroe, and stay awhile with the war chief who commanded it. But, having been so long from my people, I told him that I would rather return to my nation — that Ke-o-kuck had come here once on a visit to see him, as we had done, and he let him return again, as soon as he wished; and that I expected to be treated in the same way. He insisted, however, on our going to fortress Monroe; and as our interpreter could not understand enough of our language to interpret a speech, I concluded it was best to obey our Great Father, and say nothing contrary to his wishes.

During our stay at the city, we were called upon by many of the people, who treated us well, particularly the squaws! We visited the great *council house* of the Americans — the place where they keep their *big guns* — and all the public buildings, and then started to fortress Monroe. The war chief met us, on our arrival, and shook hands, and appeared glad to see me. He treated us with great friendship, and talked to me frequently. Previous to our leaving this fort, he gave us a feast, and made us some presents, which I intend to keep for his sake. He is a very good man, and a great *brave!* I was sorry to leave him, although I was going to return to my people, because he had treated me like a brother, during all the time I remained with him.

Having got a new guide, a war chief, [Maj. Garland,] we started for our own country, taking a circuitous route. Our Great Father being about to pay a visit to his children in the *big towns* towards sunrising, and being desirous that we should have an opportunity of seeing them, directed our guide to take us through.

On our arrival at Baltimore, we were much astonished to see so large a village; but the war chief told us that we would soon see a *larger one*. This surprised us more. During our stay here, we visited all the public buildings and places of amusement — saw much to admire, and were well entertained by the people, who crowded to see us. Our Great Father was there at the same time, and seemed to be much liked by his white children, who flocked around him, (as they had done us,) to shake him by the hand. He did not remain long—having left the city before us.[126]

We left Baltimore in a steam boat, and travelled in this way to the big village, where they make *medals* and *money*, [Philadelphia.] We again expressed surprise at finding this village so much larger than the one we had left; but the war chief again told us, that we would soon see another much larger than this. I had no idea that the white people had such large villages, and so many people. They were very kind to us—showed us all their great public works, their ships and steam boats. We visited the place where they make money, [the mint] and saw the men engaged at it. They presented each of us with a number of pieces of the *coin* as they fell from the mint, which are very handsome.

I witnessed a militia training in this city, in which were performed a number of singular military feats. The chiefs and men were well dressed, and exhibited quite a warlike appearance. I think our system of military parade far better than that of the whites—but, as I am now done going to war, I will not describe it, or say any thing more about war, or the preparations necessary for it.

We next started to New York, and on our arrival near the wharf, saw a large collection of people gathered at Castle-Garden. We had seen many wonderful sights in our way—large villages, the great *national road* over the mountains, the *rail-roads*, steam carriages, ships, steam boats, and many other things; but we were now about to witness a sight more surprising than any of these. We were told that a man was going up into the air in a balloon! We watched with anxiety to see if it could be true; and to our utter astonishment, saw him ascend in the air until the eye could no longer perceive him. Our people were all surprised, and one of our young men asked the *prophet*, if he was going up to see the Great Spirit?

[126] In the 1882 edition, Black Hawk relates here the words Jackson spoke to the Indians at Baltimore. It is a verbatim copy of the quotation which appeared in several newspapers at the time, e.g., *Niles' Weekly Register*, 8 (1833) 256. Patterson may have obtained the quotation from this source or from B. Drake, who reprinted it in 1838.

After the ascension of the balloon, we landed, and got into a carriage, to go to the house that had been provided for our reception. We had proceeded but a short distance, before the street was so crowded that it was impossible for the carriage to pass. The war chief then directed the coachman to take another street, and stop at a different house from the one he had intended. On our arrival here, we were waited upon by a number of gentlemen, who seemed much pleased to see us. We were furnished with good rooms, good provisions, and every thing necessary for our comfort.

The chiefs of this *big village*, being desirous that all their people should have an opportunity to see us, fitted up their great *council-house* for this purpose, where we saw an immense number of people; all of whom treated us with friendship, and many with great generosity.[127]

The chiefs were particular in showing us every thing that they thought would be pleasing or gratifying to us. We went with them to Castle-Garden to see the fireworks, which was quite an agreeable entertainment — but to the *whites* who witnessed it, less *magnificent* than the sight of one of our large *prairies* would be when on fire.

We visited all the public buildings and places of amusement, which to us were truly astonishing, yet very gratifying.

Every body treated us with friendship, and many with great liberality. The squaws presented us many handsome little presents, that are said to be valuable. They were very kind, very good, and very pretty — for *pale faces!*

Among the men who treated us with marked friendship, by the presentation of many valuable presents, I cannot omit to mention the name of my old friend, CROOKS, of the American Fur Company.[128] I have known him long, and have always found him to be a good chief — one who gives good advice, and treats our people

---

[127] Here the 1882 edition contains this statement: "One of their great chiefs, John A. Graham, waited upon us and made a very pretty talk, which appeared in the village papers, one of which I now hand you." Graham's speech then follows.

[128] Ramsay Crooks (1787–1859), a powerful figure in the American fur trade. He was a partner of John Jacob Astor, and upon Astor's retirement he became president of the northern independent branch of the company.

right. I shall always be proud to recognize him as a friend, and glad to shake him by the hand.

Having seen all the wonders of this *big village*, and being anxious to return to our people, our guide started with us for our own country. On arriving at Albany, the people were so anxious to see us, that they crowded the street and wharves, where the steam boat landed, so much, that it was almost impossible for us to pass to the hotel which had been provided for our reception.

We remained here but a short time, and then started for Detroit. I had spent many pleasant days at this place; and anticipated, on my arrival, to meet many of my old friends — but in this I was disappointed. What could be the cause of this? Are they all dead? Or what has become of them? I did not see our old father [129] there, who had always gave me good advice, and treated me with friendship.

After leaving Detroit, it was but a few days before we landed at Prairie du Chien. The war chief at the fort treated us very kindly, as did the people generally. I called on the father of the Winnebagoes, [Gen. J. M. Street,] [130] to whom I had surrendered myself after the battle at the Bad Axe, who received me very friendly. I told him that I had left my great *medicine bag* with his chiefs before I gave myself up; and now, that I was to enjoy my liberty again, I was anxious to get it, that I might hand it down to my nation unsullied!

He said it was safe; he had heard his chiefs speak of it, and would get it and send it to me. I hope he will not forget his promise, as the whites generally do — because I have always heard that he was a good man, and a good father — and made no promises that he did not fulfil.

Passing down the Mississippi, I discovered a large collection of

[129] Gov. Lewis Cass.
[130] Joseph Montfort Street (1782–1840), who became Indian agent to the Winnebago at Prairie du Chien in 1827. He had been publisher of the *Western World*, in Frankfort, Kentucky, then had moved to Illinois where he became active in local politics. He was a brigadier general in the Illinois militia. As Indian agent he usually was a strong defender of Indian rights, and both Jackson and Van Buren refused to remove him from office in the face of pressure from his political opponents.

people in the mining country, on the west side of the river, *and on the ground that we had given to our relation,* DUBUQUE,[131] *a long time ago.* I was surprised at this, as I had understood from our Great Father, that the Mississippi was to be the dividing line between his red and white children, and that he did not wish *either* to *cross it.* I was much pleased with this talk, as I knew that it would be much better for both parties. I have since found the country much settled by the whites further down, and near to our people, on the west side of the river. I am very much afraid, that in a few years, they will begin to drive and abuse our people, as they have formerly done. I may not live to *see* it, but I feel certain that the day is not distant.

When we arrived at Rock Island, Ke-o-kuck and the other chiefs were sent for. They arrived the next day with a great number of their young men, and came over to see me. I was pleased to see them, and they all appeared glad to see me. Among them were some who had lost relations during the war the year before. When we met, I perceived the tear of sorrow gush from their eyes at the recollection of their loss; yet they exhibited a smiling countenance, from the joy they felt at seeing me alive and well.

The next morning the war chief, our guide, convened a council at fort Armstrong. Ke-o-kuck and his party went to the fort; but, in consequence of the war chief not having called for me to accompany him, I concluded that I would wait until I was sent for. Consequently the interpreter came, and said, "they were ready, and had been waiting for me to come to the fort." I told him I was ready, and would accompany him. On our arrival there, the council commenced. The war chief said that the object of this council was to deliver me up to Ke-o-kuck. He then read a paper, and *directed me to follow Ke-o-kuck's advice, and be governed by his counsel in all things!* In this speech he said much that was mortifying to my feelings, and I made an *indignant reply.*

I do not know what object the war chief had in making such a

---

[131] Julien Dubuque (1762–1810), first white man to settle in Iowa, had received sole permission from the Fox in 1788 to work the lead mines on the west side of the river, where Dubuque, Iowa, now stands. He operated the mines and traded in furs for twenty years, until his enterprise fell into the hands of creditors.

speech, or whether he intended what he said; but I do know, that it was uncalled for, and did not become him. I have addressed many war chiefs, and have listened to their speeches with pleasure — but never had my feelings of pride and honor insulted on any former occasion. I am sorry that I was so hasty in reply to this chief, because I said that which I did not intend.[132]

In this council, I met my old friend, a great war chief, [Col. WM. DAVENPORT,][133] whom I had known about eighteen years. He is a good and brave chief. He always treated me well, and gave me good advice. He made a speech to me on this occasion, very different from that of the other chief. It sounded like coming from a *brave!* He said he had known me a long time — that we had been good friends during that acquaintance — and, although he had fought against my braves, in our late war, he still extended the hand of friendship to me — and hoped, that I was now satisfied, from what I had seen in my travels, that it was folly to think of going to war against the whites, and would ever remain at peace. He said he would be glad to see me at all times — and on all occasions would be happy to give me good advice.

If our Great Father were to make such men our agents, he would much better subserve the interests of *our* people, as well as *his own*, than in any other way. The war chiefs all know our people, and are respected by them. If the war chiefs, at the different military posts on the frontiers, were made agents, they could always prevent difficulties from arising among the Indians and whites; and I have no doubt, had the war chief above alluded to, been our agent, we never would have had the difficulties with the whites

[132] The war chief, Maj. John Garland, later described the incident this way: "In Council, Black Hawk shewed some emotion, when the Chiefs and Warriors, by whom he was surrounded, were given to understand, that Keokuck was looked to as the head of the Nation. The old man rose to speak, but was so much agitated and embarrassed, that he said but few words, expressive of dissatisfaction, and sat down; He, however, soon discovered, that he had gone too far, and begged, that what he had said, might be forgotten, that he did not mean it and did not wish it to reach the ears of the President, for he had given him his word that he would remain at peace and he intended to do it." (Garland to the Secretary of War, Oct. 5, 1833, NA:OIA.)
[133] A regular Army officer then in command of Fort Armstrong, and not to be confused with Col. George Davenport, the trader.

which we have had. Our agents ought always to be *braves!* I would, therefore, recommend to our Great Father, the propriety of breaking up the present Indian establishment, and creating a new one — and of making the commanding officers, at the different frontier posts, the agents of the government for the different nations of Indians.

I have a good opinion of the American war chiefs, generally, with whom I am acquainted; and my people, who had an opportunity of seeing and becoming well acquainted with the great war chief, [Gen. WINFIELD SCOTT,] who made the last treaty with them, in conjunction with the great chief of Illinois, [Governor REYNOLDS,] all tell me that he is the *greatest brave* they ever saw, and a good man — one who fulfils all his promises. Our braves speak more highly of him, than any chief that has ever been among us, or made treaties with us. Whatever he says, may be depended upon. If he had been our Great Father, we never would have been *compelled* to join the British in their last war with America — and I have thought that, as our Great Father is changed every few years, that his children would do well to put this great war chief in his place — as they cannot find a better chief for a Great Father any where.

I would be glad if the *village criers,* [editors,] in all the villages I passed through, would let their people know my wishes and opinions about this great war chief.

During my travels, my opinions were asked on different subjects — but for want of a good interpreter, were very seldom given. Presuming that they would be equally acceptable now, I have thought it a part of my duty, to lay the most important before the public.

The subject of colonizing the *negroes* was introduced, and my opinion asked, as to the best method of getting clear of these people. I was not prepared, at the time, to answer — as I knew but little about their situation. I have since made many inquiries on the subject — and find that a number of states admit no slaves, whilst the balance hold these negroes as slaves, and are anxious, but do not know, how to get clear of them. I will now give my plan, which, when understood, I hope will be adopted.

Let the free states remove all the *male* negroes within their limits, to the slave states — then let our Great Father buy all the *female* negroes in the slave states, between the ages of twelve and twenty, and sell them to the people of the free states, for a term of years — say, those under fifteen, until they are twenty-one — and those of, and over fifteen, for five years — and continue to buy all the females in the slave states, as soon as they arrive at the age of twelve, and take them to the free states, and dispose of them in the same way as the first — and it will not be long before the country is clear of the *black skins*, about which, I am told, they have been talking, for a long time; and for which they have expended a large amount of money.

I have no doubt but our Great Father would willingly do his part in accomplishing this object for his children — as he could not lose much by it, and would make them all happy. If the free states did not want them all for servants, we would take the balance in our nation, to help our women make corn!

I have not time now, nor is it necessary, to enter more into detail about my travels through the United States. The white people know all about them, and my people have started to their hunting grounds, and I am anxious to follow them.

Before I take leave of the public, I must contradict the story of some *village criers*, who (I have been told,) accuse me of "having murdered women and children among the whites!" This assertion is *false!* I never did, nor have I any knowledge that any of my nation ever killed a white woman or child. I make this statement of truth, to satisfy the white people among whom I have been travelling, (and by whom I have been treated with great kindness,) that, when they shook me by the hand so cordially, they did not shake the hand that had ever been raised against any but warriors.

It has always been our custom to receive all strangers that come to our village or camps, in time of peace, to share with them the best provisions we have, and give them all the assistance in our power. If on a journey, or lost, to put them on the right trail — and if in want of mocasins, to supply them. I feel grateful to the whites for the kind manner they treated me and my party, whilst travelling among them — and from my heart I assure them, that the white man will always be welcome in our village or camps, as a brother. The tomahawk is buried forever! We will forget what has past — and may the watchword between the Americans and Sacs and Foxes, ever be — *"Friendship!"*

I am now done. A few more moons, and I must follow my fathers to the shades! May the Great Spirit keep our people and the whites always at peace — is the sincere wish of

BLACK HAWK.

epilogue: *an old frock coat and brown hat*

Black Hawk lived for five years after the publication of his autobiography. During most of this time his home was a lodge of peeled bark near the Iowa River. Residing with him were his wife, two sons, and a daughter named Namequa who was handsome enough to compete with local white girls for the glances of young pioneer men.

Cutting Marsh, a missionary who visited the Sauk and Fox in 1834, described Black Hawk's lodge as "a specimen of neatness and good order," surrounded by melon vines. The old man was away when Marsh called, but his children were polite hosts. (*Wis. Hist. Coll.*, 15:117.)

Less receptive to the missionary's preaching was Keokuk, now the undisputed leader of the Sauk and Fox. Marsh complained that the chief had little patience with Christian ministers. But although Keokuk resisted the white man's religion, he was forced to accept the white man's way of doing business; credit became more and more essential to the tribes as their traditional economy dissolved. At last, when they were deep in debt and living largely on annuities, the Sauk and Fox decided to sell four hundred square miles of Keokuk's area for payment of debts.

At the ceremony of Sept. 27, 1836, transferring the lands, George Catlin was present. He wrote, "The poor dethroned monarch, old Black Hawk, was present, and looked an object of pity. With an old frock coat and brown hat on, and a cane in his hand, he stood the whole time outside of the group, and in dumb and dismal silence. . . ." (Catlin, 217.)

This serious loss of land was still not enough to stave off the inevitable press of civilization. In 1837 a million and a quarter acres adjoining the 1836 cession were sold in a transaction that required a delegation to visit Washington. Black Hawk was a member of this group, and though he was not lionized as he had been in 1833 he still was an object of attention throughout the East. Once more he sat for artist Charles Bird King, the prolific creator of Indian portraits. But Keokuk was the leader of the group — and a colorful one.

In 1838 Black Hawk and his family moved to a new home along the Des Moines River. When he was honored at an Independence Day celebration in Fort Madison that year, he could not resist one last complaint against Keokuk. "I was once a great warrior," he said. "I am now poor. Keokuk has been the cause of my present situation."

After Black Hawk's death, Oct. 3, 1838, he was buried above ground in the traditional manner — sitting erect inside a small mausoleum of logs. But his bones were not to rest there long: the grave was soon robbed. Eventually his remains were deposited in the museum of the Geological and Historical Society, Burlington, Iowa, and were destroyed when the building burned in 1855.

The agent who supervised Black Hawk in these last years was Joseph M. Street, the man who — in accordance with government policy — had alerted the Sioux when Black Hawk's people were struggling toward the Mississippi before the battle of the Bad Axe. Street was now in charge of the Sauk and Fox agency at Rock Island. He gave Black Hawk a cow and apparently was respected by the waning old man.

At about this time, Street estimated the population of the Sauk and Fox, excluding those living on the Missouri, at 4,396, "inhabiting a fertile and well watered country." And he said, "These Indians have the most flattering prospects of doing well and living happy." (Galland, *Iowa Emigrant*, 13–14.) But Street was too optimistic: by 1842 the Indians had consented to exchange their Iowa lands for an area in Kansas. About 1857–59 the two tribes disagreed and separated, and the Fox returned to Iowa to settle at Tama, on the Iowa River. In 1867 the Sauk ceded their Kansas lands and moved to the Indian Territory. In 1937 the Fox population in Iowa was 441; the Sauk numbered 987, mostly in Oklahoma.

appendix 1

Treaty of 1804
(From Kappler, *Laws and Treaties*, II, 54–56)

ARTICLES of a treaty made at St. Louis in the district of Louisiana between William Henry Harrison, governor of the Indiana territory and of the district of Louisiana, superintendant of Indian affairs for the said territory and district, and commissioner plenipotentiary of the United States for concluding any treaty or treaties which may be found necessary with any of the north western tribes of Indians of the one part, and the chiefs and head men of the united Sac and Fox tribes of the other part.

ARTICLE 1. The United States receive the united Sac and Fox tribes into their friendship and protection, and the said tribes agree to consider themselves under the protection of the United States, and of no other power whatsoever.

ART. 2. The general boundary line between the lands of the United States and of the said Indian tribes shall be as follows, to wit: Beginning at a point on the Missouri river opposite to the mouth of the Gasconade river; thence in a direct course so as to strike the river Jeffreon at the distance of thirty miles from its mouth, and down the said Jeffreon to the Mississippi, thence up the Mississippi to the mouth of the Ouisconsing river and up the same to a point which shall be thirty-six miles in a direct line from the mouth of the said river, thence by a direct line to the point where the Fox river (a branch of the Illinois) leaves the small lake called Sakaegan, thence down the Fox river to the Illinois river, and down the same to the Mississippi. And the said tribes, for and in consideration of the friendship and protection of the United States which is now extended to them, of the goods (to the value of two thousand two hundred and thirty-four dollars and fifty cents) which are now delivered, and of the annuity hereinafter stipulated to be paid, do hereby cede and relinquish forever to the United States, all the lands included within the above-described boundary.

ART. 3. In consideration of the cession and relinquishment of land made in the preceding article, the United States will deliver to the said tribes at the town of St. Louis or some other convenient place on the Mississippi yearly and every year goods suited to the circumstances of the Indians of the value of one thousand dollars (six hundred of which are intended for the Sacs and four hundred for the Foxes) reckoning that value at the first cost of the goods in the city or place in the United States where they shall be procured. And if the said tribes shall hereafter at an annual delivery of the goods aforesaid, desire that a part of their annuity should be furnished in domestic animals, implements of husbandry and other utensils convenient for them, or in compensation to useful artificers who may reside with or near them, and be employed for their benefit, the same shall at the subsequent annual delivery be furnished accordingly.

ART. 4. The United States will never interrupt the said tribes in the possession of the lands which they rightfully claim, but will on the contrary protect them in the quiet enjoyment of the same against their own citizens and against all other white persons who may intrude upon them. And the said tribes do hereby engage that they will never sell their lands or any part thereof to any sovereign power, but the United States, nor to the citizens or subjects of any other sovereign power, nor to the citizens of the United States.

ART. 5. Lest the friendship which is now established between the United States and the said Indian tribes should be interrupted by the misconduct of individuals, it is hereby agreed that for injuries done by individuals no private revenge or retaliation shall take place, but, instead thereof, complaints shall be made by the party injured to the other — by the said tribes or either of them to the superintendent of Indian affairs or one of his deputies, and by the superintendent or other person appointed by the President, to the chiefs of the said tribes. And it shall be the duty of the said chiefs upon complaint being made as aforesaid to deliver up the person or persons against whom the complaint is made, to the end that he or they may be punished agreeably to the laws of the state or territory where the offence may have been committed; and in like manner if any robbery, violence or murder shall be committed on any Indian or Indians belonging to the said tribes or either of them, the person or persons so offending shall be tried, and if found guilty, punished in the like manner as if the injury had been done to a white man. And it is further agreed, that the chiefs of said tribes shall, to the utmost of their power exert themselves to recover horses or other property which may be stolen from any citizen or citizens of the United States by any individual or individuals of their tribes, and the property so recovered shall be forthwith delivered to the superintendent or other person authorized to receive it, that it may be restored to the proper owner; and in cases where the exertions of the chiefs shall be ineffectual in recovering the property stolen as aforesaid, if sufficient proof can be obtained that such property was actually stolen by any Indian or Indians belonging to said tribes or either of them, the United States may deduct from the annuity of the said tribes a sum equal to the value of the property which has been stolen. And the United States hereby guarantee to any Indian or Indians of the said tribes a full indemnification for any horses or other property which may be stolen from them by any of their citizens; provided that the property so stolen cannot be recovered and that sufficient proof is produced that it was actually stolen by a citizen of the United States.

ART. 6. If any citizen of the United States or other white person should form a settlement upon lands which are the property of the Sac and Fox tribes, upon complaint being made thereof to the superintendent or other person having charge of the affairs of the Indians, such intruder shall forthwith be removed.

ART. 7. As long as the lands which are now ceded to the United States remain their property, the Indians belonging to the said tribes, shall enjoy the privilege of living and hunting upon them.

ART. 8. As the laws of the United States regulating trade and intercourse with the Indian tribes, are already extended to the country inhabited by the Saukes and Foxes, and as it is provided by those laws that no person shall reside as a trader in the Indian country without a license under the hand [and] seal of the superintendent of Indian affairs, or other person appointed for the purpose by the President, the said tribes do promise and agree that they will not suffer any trader to reside amongst them without such license; and that they will from time to time give notice to the superintendent or to the agent for their tribes of all the traders that may be in their country.

ART. 9. In order to put a stop to the abuses and impositions which are practiced upon the said tribes by the private traders, the United States will at a convenient time establish a trading house or factory where the individuals of the said tribes can be supplied with goods at a more reasonable rate than they have been accustomed to procure them.

ART. 10. In order to evince the sincerity of their friendship and affection for the United States and a respectful deference for their advice by an act which will not only be acceptable to them but to the common Father of all the nations of the earth; the said tribes do hereby solemnly promise and agree that they will put an end to the bloody war which has heretofore raged between their tribes and those of the Great and Little Osages. And for the purpose of burying the tomahawk and renewing the friendly intercourse between themselves and the Osages, a meeting of their respective chiefs shall take place, at which under the direction of the above-named commissioner or the agent of Indian affairs residing at St. Louis, an adjustment of all their differences shall be made and peace established upon a firm and lasting basis.

ART. 11. As it is probable that the government of the United States will establish a military post at or near the mouth of the Ouisconsing river; and as the land on the lower side of the river may not be suitable for that purpose, the said tribes hereby agree that a fort may be built either on the upper side of the Ouisconsing or on the right bank of the Mississippi, as the one or the other may be found most convenient; and a tract of land not exceeding two miles square shall be given for that purpose. And the said tribes do further agree, that they will at all times allow to traders and other persons travelling through their country under the authority of the United States a free and safe passage for themselves and their property of every description. And that for such passage they shall at no time and on no account whatever be subject to any toll or exaction.

ART. 12. This treaty shall take effect and be obligatory on the contracting parties as soon as the same shall have been ratified by the President by and with the advice and consent of the Senate of the United States.

ADDITIONAL ARTICLE

It is agreed that nothing in this treaty contained, shall affect the claim of any individual or individuals who may have obtained grants of land from the Spanish government, and which are not included within the general boundary line laid down in this treaty, provided that such grant have at any time been made known to the said tribes and recognized by them.

----

appendix 2

Treaty of 1832
(From a microfilm copy of an original manuscript in the Davenport, Iowa, Public Museum)

Articles of a treaty of peace, friendship and cession concluded, at Fort Armstrong, Rock Island Illinois, between the United States of America, by their commissioners Major General Winfield Scott, of the United States Army, and his Excellency John Reynolds, Governor of the state of Illinois, and the confederated tribes of Sac and Fox Indians, repre-sented, in General Council, by the undersigned Chiefs, Head-Men, and Warriors.

Whereas, under certain lawless and desperate leaders a formidable band, constituting a large portion of the Sac and Fox nation, left their country in April last, and, in violation of treaties, commenced an unprovoked war upon unsuspecting and defenceless citizens of the United States, sparing neither age nor sex; and whereas, the United States, at a great expense of treasure have subdued the said hostile band, killing or cap-turing all its principal Chiefs and Warriors — the said States, partly as indemnity for the expense incurred, and partly to secure the future safety and tranquility of the invaded frontier, demand of the said tribes, to the use of the United States, a cession of a tract of the Sac and Fox country, bordering on said frontier, more than proportional to the numbers of the hostile band who have been so conquered and subdued.

Article 1 — Accordingly, the confederated tribes of Sacs and Foxes hereby cede to the United States forever, all the lands to which the said tribes have title, or claim, (with the exception of the reservation hereinafter made,) included within the following bounds, to wit: Beginning on the Mississippi river, at the point where the Sac and Fox northern boundary line, as established by the second article of the treaty of Prairie du Chien, of the fifteenth of July one thousand eight hundred and thirty, strikes said river; thence, up said boundary line to a point fifty miles from the Mississippi, measured on said line: thence, in a right line to the nearest point on the Red Cedar of the Ioway, forty miles from the Mississippi river; thence, in a right line to a point in the northern boundary line of the State of Missouri, fifty miles, measured on said boundary, from the Mississippi river; thence, by the last mentioned boundary to the Mississippi river, and by the western shore of said river to the place of beginning. And the said confederated tribes of Sacs and Foxes hereby stipulate and agree to remove from the lands herein ceded to the United States, on, or before, the first day of June next; and, in order to prevent any future misunderstanding, it is expressly understood, that no band or party of the Sac or Fox tribes shall reside, plant, fish, or hunt on any portion of the ceded country after the period just mentioned.

Article 2d. Out of the cession made in the preceding article, the United States agree to a reservation, for the use of the said confederated tribes, of a tract of land containing four hundred square miles, to be laid off, under the directions of the President of the United States, from the boundary line crossing the Ioway river, in such manner that nearly an equal portion of the reservation may be on both sides of said river, and extending downwards so as to include Ke-o-kuck's principal village on its right bank, which village is about twelve miles from the Mississippi river.

Article 3d. In consideration of the great extent of the foregoing cession, the United States stipulate and agree to pay to the said confederated tribes, annually, for thirty successive years, the first payment to be made in September of the next year, the sum of twenty thousand dollars in specie.

Article 4th. It is further agreed that the United States shall establish and maintain within the limits, and for the use and benefit of the Sacs and Foxes, for the period of thirty years, one additional Black and Gun Smith shop, with the necessary tools, iron and steel; and finally make a yearly allowance for the same period, to the said tribes, of forty kegs of tobacco, and forty barrels of salt, to be delivered at the mouth of the Iowa river.

Article 5th. The United States, at the earnest request of the said confederated tribes, further agree to pay to Farnham and Davenport, Indian traders at Rock Island, the sum of forty thousand dollars, without interest, which sum will be in full satisfaction of the claims of the said traders against the said tribes, and by the latter was, on the tenth day of July, one thousand eight hundred and thirty-one, acknowledged to be justly due, for articles of necessity furnished in the course of the seven preceding years, in an instrument of writing of said date, duly signed by the Chiefs and head-men of said tribes, and certified by the late Felix St Vrain United States' Agent and Antoine Le Claire United States' Interpreter, both for the said tribes.

Article 6th. At the special request of the said confederated tribes, the United States agree to grant, by patent, in fee simple, to Antoine Le Claire, Interpreter a part Indian, one section of land opposite Rock Island, and one section at the head of the first rapids above said Island, within the country herein ceded by the Sacs & Foxes.

Article 7th. Trusting to the good faith of the neutral bands of Sacs and Foxes, the United States have already delivered up to those bands the great mass of prisoners made in the course of war by the United States and promise to use their influence to procure the delivery of other Sacs and Foxes who may still be prisoners in the hands of a band of Sioux Indians, the friends of the United States; but the following named prisoners of war, now in confinement who were Chiefs and head-men, shall be held as hostages, for the future good conduct of the late hostile bands during the pleasure of the President of the United States, viz; — Muk-ka-ta-mish-a-ka-kaik (or *Black Hawk*) and his two sons; Wau-ba-kee-shiek (*the Prophet*) his brother and two sons; Napope; We-sheet; Ioway; Pama-ho and Cha-kee-pa-shi-pa-ho (*the Little Stabbing* Chief.)

Article 8th. And it is further stipulated and agreed between the parties to this treaty, that there shall never be allowed in the confederated Sac & Fox nations, any separate band or village under any chief or warrior of the large hostile bands; but that the remnant of the said hostile bands shall be divided among the neutral bands of the said tribes according to blood — the Sacs among the Sacs, and the Foxes among the Foxes.

Article 9th. In consideration of the premises peace and friendship are declared and shall be perpetually maintained between the United States and the whole confederated Sac and Fox nation, excepting from the latter the hostages before mentioned.

Article 10th. The United States, besides the presents, delivered at the signing of this treaty, wishing to give a striking evidence of their mercy & liberality, will immediately cause to be issued to the said confederated tribes, principally for the use of the Sac and Fox women and children whose husbands, fathers and brothers have been killed in the late war, and generally for the use of the whole confederated tribes, articles of subsistence as follows: thirty five beef cattle; twelve bushels of salt; thirty barrels of pork and fifty barrels of flour; and will cause to be delivered for the same purposes in the month of April next, at the mouth of the lower Ioway, six thousand bushels of maize or Indian corn.

Article 11th. At the request of the said confederated tribes, it is agreed that a suitable present shall be made to them, on their pointing out to any

United States Agent, authorized for the purpose, the position or positions of one, or more mines, supposed by the said tribes to be of a metal more valuable than lead or iron.

Article 12th. This treaty shall take effect, and be obligatory on the contracting parties, as soon as the same shall be ratified by the President of the United States, by and with the advice and consent of the Senate thereof.

Done at Fort Armstrong Rock Island, Illinois, this twenty first day of September, in the year of our lord one thousand eight hundred and thirty two, and of the independence of the United States the fifty seventh.

bibliography

Symbol	Document Sources
CHI	Chicago Historical Society. Manuscript and print collections.
IHI	Illinois State Historical Library. Black Hawk War collection of about 1,100 documents, augmented by 900 or more in photostat and microfilm from the National Archives.
ICC	Indian Claims Commission. Testimony, Sac and Fox Tribe of Oklahoma, *et al.*, v. United States, Docket 83, 1953. Mimeographed copy in the Illinois State Historical Library.
MO	Missouri Historical Society.
NA	National Archives. Material found in the following files:
AGO	Adjutant General's Office
OIA	Office of Indian Affairs
SW	Office of the Secretary of War
WHI	State Historical Society of Wisconsin. Thomas Forsyth papers (Series T) in the Draper collection.

Books and Articles

Aldrich, Charles. "Jefferson Davis and Black Hawk," *Midland Monthly*, 5 (1896) 406–11.

Alexander, Edward P. "An Art Gallery in Frontier Wisconsin," *Wisconsin Magazine of History*, 29 (1946) 281–300.

American State Papers. Foreign Relations. 6 vols. Washington, 1832–61. Indian Affairs. 2 vols. Washington, 1832–34. Military Affairs. 7 vols. Washington, 1832–61. Miscellaneous. 2 vols. Washington, 1834. Public Lands. 8 vols. Washington, 1832–61.

An Account of the Indian Chief Black Hawk and his Tribes, the Sac and Fox Indians, with the Affecting Narrative of a Lady who was Taken Prisoner by the Indians. . . . Philadelphia, 1834.

Anderson, Gen. Robert. "Reminiscences of the Black Hawk War," *Wisconsin Historical Collections*, 19 (1888) 169–72.

Armstrong, Perry A. *The Sauks and the Black Hawk War*. Springfield, Ill., 1887.

Atwater, Caleb. *Remarks Made on a Tour to Prairie du Chien*. Columbus, Ohio, 1831.

Barbarities of the Enemy, Exposed in a Report of the Committee of the House of Representatives. . . . Troy [N. Y.], 1813.

Bassett, John Spenser, ed. *Correspondence of Andrew Jackson*. Washington, 1931.

Black Hawk. *Life of Ma-ka-tai-me-she-kia-kiak or Black Hawk*. Cincinnati, 1833. Reissued in Boston, 1834 (two editions); London, 1836; Cooperstown, 1842; Leeuwarden, Netherlands (trans.), 1847; Chicago, 1916; Iowa City, 1932.

———. *Autobiography of Ma-ka-tai-me-she-kia-kiak, or Black Hawk*. Oquawka, Ill., 1882. Reissued in Rock Island, Ill., 1912.

Carter, Clarence Edwin, ed. *The Territorial Papers of the United States*. 20 vols. Washington, D. C., 1934–.

Champlain Society. *Publications*. Toronto, Canada, 1907–.

Cole, Cyrenus. *I Am a Man: The Indian Black Hawk*. Iowa City, 1938.

Coues, Elliot, ed. *The Expeditions of Zebulon Montgomery Pike . . . during the Years 1805–6–7*. 3 vols. New York, 1895.

Cruikshank, Ernest A. "The Employment of Indians in the War of 1812," *Report of the American Historical Association*, 1895, pp. 321–35.

Drake, Benjamin F. *The Life and Adventures of Black Hawk*. Cincinnati, 1838.

Drake, Samuel G. *The Aboriginal Races of North America*. 15th ed. New York, 1880.

Esarey, Logan, ed. *Governors' Messages and Letters: Messages and Letters of William Henry Harrison*. Indiana Historical Collections. Indianapolis, 1922.

Ewers, John C. "Charles Bird King, Painter of Indian Visitors to the Nation's Capital," *Annual Report of the Smithsonian Institution for 1953*, pp. 463–73.

Ford, Thomas. *A History of Illinois*. Chicago, 1854.

Galland, Isaac. *Chronicles of the North American Savage*, May–Sept., 1835.

————. *Galland's Iowa Emigrant.* Chillicothe [Ohio], 1840. Reprinted, Iowa City, n.d.

Godwin, Parke, ed. *Prose Writings of William Cullen Bryant.* 2 vols. New York, 1901.

Greene, E. B., and C. W. Alvord, eds. *Governors' Letter-Books, 1818–1834.* Collections of the Illinois State Historical Library, Vol. 4. Springfield, 1909.

Hagan, William Thomas. *Black Hawk's Route through Wisconsin.* Mimeographed publication of the State Historical Society of Wisconsin. Madison, 1949.

Hamilton, Holman. "Zachary Taylor and the Black Hawk War," *Wisconsin Magazine of History,* 24 (1941) 305–15.

Harrington, M. R. *Sacred Bundles of the Sac and Fox Indians.* Univ. of Penn. Anthropological Pub., Vol. 4, No. 2. Philadelphia, 1914.

History of Mercer and Henderson Counties. Chicago, 1882.

Hodge, Frederick Webb, ed. *Handbook of American Indians North of Mexico.* Bulletin 30, Bureau of American Ethnology. 2 vols. Washington, D. C., 1907–10.

Kappler, Charles J., ed. *Indian Affairs. Laws and Treaties.* 2 vols. Washington, D. C., 1904. Published as U. S. Serials 4623–24.

Latrobe, Charles J. *The Rambler in North America.* 2 vols. London, 1835.

"Life of Black Hawk," a review in *North American Review,* 40 (1835) 68–87.

"Life of Ma-ka-tai-me-she-kia-kiak, or Black Hawk," a review in *American Quarterly Review,* 35 (1834) 426–48.

McCall, George A. *Letters From the Frontiers.* Philadelphia, 1868.

McKenney, Thomas L., and James Hall. *History of the Indian Tribes of North America.* 3 vols. Philadelphia, 1836–44. The edition cited was edited by Frederick Webb Hodge, 3 vols., published in Edinburgh, 1933–34.

Marshall, Thomas Maitland, ed. *The Life and Papers of Frederick Bates.* St. Louis, 1926.

Matson, N. *Memories of Shaubena.* Chicago, 1878.

Morse, Jedidiah. *A Report to the Secretary of War of the United States on Indian Affairs.* New Haven, 1822.

Pratt, Harry E. *Lincoln, 1809–1839,* in the *Lincoln Day by Day* series, Springfield, Ill., 1941.

Reynolds, John. *My Own Times.* Chicago, 1879.

Royce, Charles C., compiler. *Indian Land Cessions of the United States.* Eighteenth Annual Report, Bureau of American Ethnology. Washington, D. C., 1896–97.

Scanlan, P. L. "The Military Record of Jefferson Davis in Wisconsin," *Wisconsin Magazine of History,* 24 (1940) 174–82.

Schoolcraft, Henry R. *Personal Memoirs of a Residence of Thirty Years with the Indian Tribes on the American Frontiers.* Philadelphia, 1851.

Scripps, James E. *Memorials of the Scripps Family: A Centennial Tribute.* Detroit, 1891.

Snyder, Charles. "Antoine LeClaire, the First Proprietor of Davenport," *Annals of Iowa,* 3rd ser., 23 (1941–42) 79–117.

Stevens, Frank E. *The Black Hawk War.* Chicago, 1903.

Swanton, John R. *The Indian Tribes of North America.* Bulletin 145, Bureau of American Ethnology. Washington, 1952.

Thwaites, Reuben Gold, ed. *Early Western Travels, 1748–1846.* 32 vols. Cleveland, 1904–7.

Tucker, Sara Jones, compiler. *Indian Villages of the Illinois Country.* 2 vols. Springfield, Ill., 1942.

Wakefield, John A. *History of the War between the United States and the Sac and Fox Nations.* . . . Jacksonville, Ill., 1834.

index